HARRAP

FRENCH GRAMMAR

Compiled by
LEXUS

with
Raymond Perrez
Noël Peacock
Sabine Citron

D0434559

HARRAP

This edition published by Chambers Harrap Publishers Ltd 2002
7 Hopetoun Crescent, Edinburgh, EH7 4AY

Previous edition published 1987

ISBN 0245 60706 4

Reprinted 2004 (twice)

Designed and typeset by Chambers Harrap Publishers Ltd
Printed in Great Britain by Clays Ltd, St Ives plc

INTRODUCTION

This French grammar has been written to meet the new demands of language teaching in schools and colleges and is particularly suitable for exam revision. The essential rules of the French language have been set in terms that are as accessible as possible to all users. Where technical terms have been used, then full explanations of these terms have also been supplied. There is also a full glossary of grammatical terminology on pages 7-14. While literary aspects of the French language have not been ignored, the emphasis has been placed squarely on modern spoken French. This grammar, with its wealth of lively and typical illustrations of usage taken from the present-day language, is the ideal study tool for all levels – from the beginner who is starting to come to grips with the French language through to the advanced user who requires a comprehensive and readily accessible work of reference.

Abbreviations used in the text:

fem	feminine
masc	masculine
plur	plural
sing	singular

CONTENTS

CONTENTS

1. GLOSSARY OF GRAMMATICAL TERMS

ADJECTIVE

An adjective provides supplementary information about a noun, describing what something is like, eg *a **small** house, a **red** car, an **interesting** pastime*.

ADVERB

Adverbs are normally used with a verb to add extra information by indicating **how** the action is done (adverbs of manner), **when, where** or **with how much intensity** the action is done (adverbs of time, place and intensity), or **to what extent** the action is done (adverbs of quantity). Adverbs may also be used with an adjective or another adverb, eg *a **very** attractive girl, **very** well*.

AGREEMENT

In French, words such as adjectives, articles and pronouns must agree in number and gender with the noun or pronoun to which they refer. This means that their spelling changes according to the **number** of the noun (singular or plural) and according to its **gender** (masculine or feminine).

ANTECEDENT

The antecedent of a relative pronoun is the word or words to which the relative pronoun refers. The antecedent is usually found directly before the relative pronoun, eg in the sentence *I know **the man** who did this*, *the man* is the antecedent of *who*.

APPOSITION

A word or a clause is said to be in apposition to another when it is placed directly after it without any joining word, eg *Mr Jones, **our bank manager**, rang today*.

ARTICLE

See DEFINITE ARTICLE, INDEFINITE ARTICLE and PARTITIVE ARTICLE.

ASPIRATE H

If a word begins with an aspirate h in French, it means that there is no liaison between it and the word preceding it, eg in **les haricots** the **s** of **les** is not pronounced. Similarly, there is no contraction in spelling, eg **la haine** and not **l'haine**. See SILENT H.

AUXILIARY

The French auxiliary verbs are **avoir** (*to have*) and **être** (*to be*). They are used to make up the first part of compound tenses, the second part being a past participle, eg *j'ai mangé, il est allé*.

CARDINAL

Cardinal numbers are numbers such as *one, two, ten, fourteen*, as opposed to **ordinal** numbers, eg *first, second*.

CLAUSE

A clause is a group of words which contains at least a subject and a verb: *he said* is a clause. A clause often contains more than this basic information, eg *he said this to her yesterday*. Sentences can be made up of several clauses, eg *he said/he'd call me/if he were free*. See SENTENCE.

COMPARATIVE

The comparative forms of adjectives and adverbs allow two things, persons or actions to be compared. In English, *more ... than, ...er than, less ... than* and *as ... as* are used for comparison.

COMPOUND

Compound tenses are verb tenses consisting of more than one element. In French, the compound tenses of a verb are formed by the **auxiliary** verb and the **past participle**: *j'ai visité, il est venu*.

CONDITIONAL

This mood is used to describe what someone would do, or something that would happen if a condition were fulfilled, eg *I **would come** if I were well; the chair **would have broken** if he had sat on it*.

CONJUGATION

The conjugation of a verb is the set of different forms taken in the particular tenses of that verb.

CONJUNCTION

Conjunctions are used to link different clauses. They may be coordinating or subordinating. Coordinating conjunctions are words like *and, but, or*; subordinating conjunctions are words like *because, after, although*.

DEFINITE ARTICLE

The definite article is *the* in English and *le*, *la* and *les* in French.

DEMONSTRATIVE

Demonstrative adjectives such as *this, that, these* and pronouns such as *this one, that one* are used to point out a particular person or object.

DIRECT OBJECT

A direct object is a noun or a pronoun which in English follows a verb without any linking preposition, eg *I met a **friend***.

ELISION

Elision consists in replacing the last letter of certain words (*le, la, je, me, te, se, de, que*) with an apostrophe before a word starting with a **vowel** or a **silent h**, eg *l'eau, l'homme, j'aime*.

ENDING

The ending of a verb is determined by the **person** (1st/2nd/3rd) and **number** (singular/plural) of its subject. In French, most tenses have six different endings. See PERSON and NUMBER.

GLOSSARY

EXCLAMATION

An exclamation is a word or sentence used to express surprise or wonder, eg *what!, how!, how lucky!, what a nice day!*

FEMININE

See GENDER.

GENDER

The gender of a noun indicates whether the noun is **masculine** or **feminine** (all French nouns are either masculine or feminine).

IDIOMATIC EXPRESSIONS

Idiomatic expressions (or idioms) are expressions which cannot normally be translated word for word. For example, *it's raining cats and dogs* is translated by *il pleut des cordes.*

IMPERATIVE

This mood is used for giving orders, eg *eat!, don't go!*

INDEFINITE

Indefinite pronouns and adjectives are words that do not refer to a definite person or object, eg *each, someone, every.*

INDEFINITE ARTICLE

The indefinite article is *a* in English and *un, une* and *des* in French.

INDICATIVE

The indicative is the normal form of a verb as in *I like, he came, we are trying.* It is opposed to the subjunctive, conditional and imperative.

INDIRECT OBJECT

An indirect object is a pronoun or noun which follows a verb indirectly, with a linking preposition (usually **to**), eg *I spoke to **my friend/him**.*

INFINITIVE

The infinitive is the basic form of the verb as found in dictionaries. Thus *to eat*, *to finish*, *to take* are infinitives. In French, the infinitive is recognizable by its ending (**-er**, **-ir** or **-re**, eg *manger*, *finir*, *prendre*).

INTERROGATIVE

Interrogative words are used to ask a question. This may be a direct question (**when** *will you arrive?*) or an indirect question (*I don't know* **when** *he'll arrive*). See QUESTION.

MASCULINE

See GENDER.

MOOD

This is the name given to the four main areas within which a verb is conjugated. See INDICATIVE, SUBJUNCTIVE, CONDITIONAL, IMPERATIVE.

NOUN

A noun is a word or group of words which refers to a living creature, a thing, a place or an abstract idea, eg *postman, cat, shop, passport, life*.

NUMBER

The number of a noun indicates whether the noun is **singular** or **plural**. A singular noun refers to one single person or thing, eg *boy, train* and a plural noun to more than one, eg *boys, trains*.

ORDINAL

Ordinal numbers are *first, second, third, fourth* and all other numbers which end in **-th**. In French, all ordinal numbers, except for *premier* (first) and *second* (second), end in **-ième**.

PARTITIVE ARTICLE

The partitive articles are *some* and *any* in English and *du, de la, de l'* and *des* (as in *du pain, de la confiture, de l'eau, des bananes*) in French.

GLOSSARY

PASSIVE

A verb is used in the passive when the subject of the verb does not perform the action but is subjected to it. The passive is formed with the verb **to be** and the past participle of the verb, eg *he was rewarded*.

PAST PARTICIPLE

The past participle of a verb is the form which is used after **to have** in English, eg *I have **eaten**, I have **said**, you have **tried***.

PERSON

In any tense, there are three persons in the singular (1st: *I* ..., 2nd: *you* ..., 3rd: *he/she* ...), and three in the plural (1st: *we* ..., 2nd: *you* ..., 3rd: *they* ...). See also ENDING.

PERSONAL PRONOUNS

Personal pronouns stand for a noun. They usually accompany a verb and can be either the subject (*I, you, he/she/it, we, they*) or the object of the verb (*me, you, him/her/it, us, them*).

PLURAL

See NUMBER.

POSSESSIVE

Possessive adjectives and pronouns are used to indicate possession or ownership. They are words like *my/mine, your/yours, our/ours*.

PREPOSITION

Prepositions are words such as *with, in, to, at*. They are followed by a noun or a pronoun.

PRESENT PARTICIPLE

The present participle is the verb form which ends in **-ing** in English and **-ant** in French.

PRONOUN

This is a word which stands for a noun. The main categories of pronouns are:

- **Relative pronouns** (eg *who*, *which*, *that*)
- **Interrogative pronouns** (eg *who?*, *what?*, *which?*)
- **Demonstrative pronouns** (eg *this*, *that*, *these*)
- **Possessive pronouns** (eg *mine*, *yours*, *his*)
- **Personal pronouns** (eg *you*, *him*, *us*)
- **Reflexive pronouns** (eg *myself*, *himself*)
- **Indefinite pronouns** (eg *something*, *all*)

QUESTION

There are two question forms: **direct** questions stand on their own and require a question mark at the end, eg *when will he come?*; **indirect** questions are introduced by a clause and require no question mark, eg *I wonder when he will come.*

REFLEXIVE

Reflexive verbs 'reflect' the action back onto the subject, eg *I dressed myself*. They are always found with a reflexive pronoun and are much more common in French than in English.

SENTENCE

A sentence is a group of words made up of one or more clauses (see CLAUSE) and which makes a complete grammatical structure. The end of a sentence is indicated by a punctuation mark (usually a full stop, a question mark or an exclamation mark).

SILENT H

The term 'silent **h**' is actually misleading since an **h** is never pronounced in French. The point is that when a silent **h** occurs, any preceding vowel is not pronounced either. For example, the **h** in *j'habite* is silent (note the *j'*). The **h** in *je hurle*, however, is **aspirate**, and so there is no contraction in spelling.

GLOSSARY

SIMPLE TENSE

Simple tenses are tenses in which the verb consists of one word only, eg *j'habite, Maurice partira*.

SINGULAR

See NUMBER.

SUBJECT

The subject of a verb is the noun or pronoun which performs the action. In the sentences, *the train left early* and *she bought a record, the train* and *she* are the subjects.

SUBJUNCTIVE

The subjunctive is a verb form which is rarely used in English, eg *if I were you, God save the Queen*, but common in French.

SUPERLATIVE

The superlative is the form of an adjective or an adverb which, in English, is marked by *the most …, the …est* or *the least …*

TENSE

Verbs are used in tenses, which tell us whether an action takes place in the present, the past or the future.

VERB

A verb is a word which describes the performance of an action, eg *to sing, to work, to watch* or the existence of a state, eg *to be, to have, to hope*.

2. ARTICLES

A. The Definite Article

1. Forms

In English, there is only one form of the definite article: **the**. In French, there are three forms, depending on the gender and number of the noun following the article:

> □ with a masculine singular noun: **le**   ⎫
> □ with a feminine singular noun: **la**   ⎬   the
> □ with a plural noun (masc or fem): **les** ⎭

MASC SING	FEM SING	PLURAL
le chauffeur	**la secrétaire**	**les étudiants**
the driver	the secretary	the students
le salon	**la cuisine**	**les chambres**
the living-room	the kitchen	the bedrooms

Note: **le** and **la** both change to **l'** before a vowel or a silent **h**:

	MASCULINE	FEMININE
BEFORE VOWEL	**l'avion**	**l'odeur**
	the plane	the smell
BEFORE SILENT H	**l'homme**	**l'hôtesse**
	the man	the hostess

Pronunciation: the **s** of **les** is pronounced **z** when the noun following it begins with a vowel or a silent **h**.

2. Forms with the prepositions 'à' and 'de'

When the definite article is used with **à** or **de**, the following spelling changes take place:

a) *with **à** (to, at)*

à + le	→	au
à + les	→	aux

à + **la** and à + **l'** do not change

au restaurant
at/to the restaurant

aux enfants
to the children

à la plage
at/to the beach

à l'aéroport
at/to the airport

Pronunciation: the **x** of **aux** is pronounced **z** when the noun following it begins with a vowel or a silent **h**.

b) *with de (of, from)*

de + **le**	→		**du**
de + **les**	→		**des**

de + **la** and de + **l'** do not change

du directeur
of/from the manager

des chômeurs
of/from the unemployed

de la région
of/from the area

de l'usine
of/from the factory

Pronunciation: the **s** of **des** is pronounced **z** when the noun following it begins with a vowel or a silent **h**.

3. Use

As in English, the definite article is used when referring to a particular person or thing, or particular persons or things:

les amis dont je t'ai parlé
the friends I told you about

le café est prêt
the coffee is ready

However, the definite article is used far more frequently in French than in English. It is used in particular in the following cases where English uses no article:

a) *when the noun is used in a general sense*

i) to refer to all things of a kind:

vous acceptez les chèques?
do you take cheques?

le sucre est mauvais pour les dents
sugar is bad for the teeth

ii) to refer to abstract things:

le travail et les loisirs
work and leisure

la musique classique
classical music

iii) when stating likes and dislikes:

j'aime la viande mais je préfère le poisson
I like meat, but I prefer fish

je déteste les tomates
I hate tomatoes

b) *with geographical names*

i) continents, countries and areas:

le Canada Canada	**la France** France	**l'Europe** Europe
la Bretagne Brittany	**l'Afrique** Africa	**les États-Unis** the United States

But: the article **la** is omitted with the prepositions **en** and **de** when used with feminine country names:

j'habite en France
I live in France

il vient d'Italie
he comes from Italy

With masculine country names, the corresponding prepositions **à** and **de** follow the normal rules:

j'habite au Portugal/aux États-Unis
I live in Portugal/in the United States

je viens du Japon/des Pays-Bas
I come from Japan/the Netherlands

A very few country names do not require an article, eg **Panamá, Cuba, Taïwan, Singapour**.

ii) mountains, lakes and rivers:

le mont Everest
Mount Everest

le lac de Genève
Lake Geneva

c) *with names of seasons*

l'automne	autumn
l'hiver	winter
le printemps	spring
l'été	summer

But: **en automne/été/hiver**
in autumn/summer/winter

au printemps
in spring

un jour d'été
a summer's day

d) *with names of languages*

j'apprends le français
I'm learning French

But: **ce film est en anglais**
this film is in English

e) *with parts of the body*

j'ai les cheveux roux
I've got red hair

ouvrez la bouche
open your mouth

les mains en l'air!
hands up!

l'homme à la barbe noire
the man with the black beard

f) *with names following an adjective*

le petit Pierre
little Pierre

la pauvre Isabelle
poor Isabelle

g) *with titles*

le docteur Coste
Doctor Coste

le commandant Cousteau
Captain Cousteau

h) *with days of the week to express regular occurrences*

que fais-tu le samedi?
what do you do on Saturdays?

le docteur reçoit le lundi et le vendredi
the doctor sees patients on Mondays and Fridays

i) *with names of subjects or leisure activities*

les maths
maths

l'histoire et la géographie
history and geography

la natation, la lecture, le football
swimming, reading, football

j) *in expressions of price, quantity etc*

c'est combien le kilo/la douzaine/la bouteille?
how much is it for a kilo/dozen/bottle?

B. The Indefinite Article

1. Forms

In French, there are three forms of the indefinite article, depending on the number and gender of the noun it accompanies:

□ with a masculine singular noun: **un**   a
□ with a feminine singular noun: **une**   a
□ with a plural noun (masc or fem): **des**   some

Note: **des** is often not translated in English:

il y a des nuages dans le ciel
there are clouds in the sky

2. Use

a) On the whole, the French indefinite article is used in the same way as its English equivalent:

un homme	**une femme**	**des hommes/ femmes**
a man	a woman	(some) men/ women
un livre	**une tasse**	**des livres/tasses**
a book	a cup	(some) books/cups

b) However, the English indefinite article is not always translated in French:

i)   when stating someone's profession or occupation:

mon père est architecte
my father is an architect

elle est médecin
she is a doctor

Note, however, that the article is used after **c'est, c'était** etc:

c'est un acteur célèbre
he's a famous actor

ce sont des fraises
these are strawberries

ii) with nouns in apposition:

Madame Leclerc, employée de bureau
Mrs Leclerc, an office worker

iii) after **quel** in exclamations:

quel dommage!   **quelle surprise!**
what a pity!   what a surprise!

c) In negative sentences, **de** (or **d'**) is used instead of **un, une, des**:

je n'ai pas d'amis   **je n'ai plus de voiture**
I don't have any friends   I don't have a car any more

d) In French (but not in English), the indefinite article is used with abstract nouns followed by an adjective:

avec une patience remarquable
with remarkable patience

elle a fait des progrès étonnants
she's made amazing progress

Note, however, that the article is not used when there is no adjective:

avec plaisir   **sans hésitation**
with pleasure   without hesitation

C. The Partitive Article

1. Forms

There are three forms of the French partitive article, which corresponds to 'some'/'any' in English:

- with a masculine singular noun: **du**
- with a feminine singular noun: **de la**
- with plural nouns (masc or fem): **des**

du vin	**de la bière**	**des fruits**
some wine	some beer	some fruit

Note that **de l'** is used in front of masculine or feminine singular nouns beginning with a vowel or a silent **h**:

de l'argent
some money

de l'eau
some water

de l'helium
some helium

2. Use

a) On the whole, the French partitive article is used as in English. However, English tends to omit the partitive article where French does not:

achète du pain
buy (some) bread

vous avez du beurre?
do you have (any) butter?

je voudrais de la viande
I'd like some meat

tu veux de la soupe?
do you want (any) soup?

tu dois manger des légumes
you must eat (some) vegetables

as-tu acheté des poires?
did you buy any pears?

b) The partitive article is replaced by **de** (or **d'**) in the following cases:

i) in negative expressions:

il n'y a plus de café
there isn't any coffee left

je n'ai pas de frères
I don't have any brothers

nous n'avons plus d'argent
we don't have any money left

je n'ai pas d'enfants
I don't have any children

Note, however, that when the clause is introduced by **c'est, il est** etc, the partitive article remains:

ce n'est pas du cuir, c'est du plastique
it's not leather, it's plastic

ii) after expressions of quantity (see also pp 232-4):

il boit trop de café
he drinks too much coffee

il gagne assez d'argent
he earns enough money

iii) after **avoir besoin de**:

j'ai besoin d'argent
I need (some) money

tu as besoin de timbres?
do you need (any) stamps?

iv) where an adjective is followed by a plural noun:

de petites villes
(some) small towns

d'énormes mensonges
outrageous lies

Note, however, that if the adjective comes after the noun, **des** does not change:

des résultats encourageants
encouraging results

2. Partitive or definite article?

When no article is used in English, it is not always clear which is the right article in French: **le/la/les** or **du/de la/des**.

If **some/any** can be inserted before the English noun, the French partitive article should be used. But if the noun is used in a general sense and inserting **some/any** in front of the English noun does not make sense, the definite article must be used:

did you buy fish? (*ie any fish*)
tu as acheté *du* poisson?

yes, I did; I like fish (*ie fish in general*)
oui; j'aime *le* poisson

3. NOUNS

A noun is a word or group of words which refers to a person, an animal, a thing, a place or an abstract idea.

A. Gender

All French nouns are either masculine or feminine; there is no neuter as in English. Though *no absolute rule can be stated*, the gender can often be determined either by the meaning or the ending of the noun.

1. Masculine

a) *by meaning*

   i)   words referring to men and male animals:

un homme	**le boucher**	**le tigre**
a man	the butcher	the tiger

   ii)   names of common trees and shrubs:

le chêne	**le sapin**	**le laurier**
the oak	the fir tree	the laurel

   iii)   days, months, seasons:

lundi	**mars**	**le printemps**
Monday	March	spring

   iv)   languages:

le français	**le polonais**	**le russe**
French	Polish	Russian

   v)   rivers and countries not ending in a silent **e**:

le Nil	**le Portugal**	**le Danemark**
the Nile	Portugal	Denmark

Note, however, that there are exceptions to this rule:

le Danube	**le Rhône**	**le Mexique**
the Danube	the Rhone	Mexico

b) *by ending*

-acle	**le spectacle** (show) *But:* **une débâcle** (shambles)
-age	**le fromage** (cheese) *But:* **la cage** (cage), **une image** (picture), **la nage** (swimming), **la page** (page), **la** **plage** (beach), **la rage** (rage, rabies)
-é	**le marché** (market) *But:* nouns ending in **-té** and **-tié** are usually feminine (see p 27)
-eau	**le chapeau** (hat) *But:* **l'eau** (water), **la peau** (skin)
-ège	**le piège** (trap), **le collège** (secondary school)
-ème	**le thème** (theme, topic) *But:* **la crème** (cream)
-isme, -asme	**le communisme** (communism), **le tourisme** (tourism), **l'enthousiasme** (enthusiasm)
-o	**le numéro** (the number) *But:* **la dynamo** (dynamo) and most abbreviated expressions: **une auto** (car), **la météo** (weather forecast), **la photo** (photograph), **la radio** (radio), **la sténo** (shorthand), **la stéréo** (stereo)

Nouns ending in a *consonant* are usually *masculine*.

Notable exceptions are:

i) most nouns ending in **-tion, -sion, -ation, -aison, -ison**

ii) most abstract nouns ending in **-eur** (see p 27)

iii) the following nouns ending in a consonant:

la clef (key)	**la nef** (nave)
la soif (thirst)	**la faim** (hunger)
la fin (end)	**la façon** (manner)

NOUNS

la leçon (lesson)	**la boisson** (drink)
la moisson (harvest)	**la rançon** (ransom)
la mer (sea)	**la cuiller** (spoon)
la chair (flesh)	**la basse-cour** (farmyard)
la cour (yard)	**la tour** (tower)
la brebis (ewe)	**une fois** (once)
la vis (screw)	**la souris** (mouse)
la part (share)	**la plupart** (majority, most)
la dent (tooth)	**la dot** (dowry)
la forêt (forest)	**la jument** (mare)
la mort (death)	**la nuit** (night)
la croix (cross)	**la noix** (nut)
la paix (peace)	**la perdrix** (partridge)
la toux (cough)	**la voix** (voice)

2. Feminine

a) *by meaning*

i)   words referring to women and female animals:

la mère	**la bonne**	**la génisse**
the mother	the maid	the heifer

ii)   names of rivers and countries ending with a silent **e**:

la Seine	**la Russie**	**la Belgique**
the Seine	Russia	Belgium

iii)   saints' days and festivals:

la Toussaint	**la Pentecôte**
All Saints' Day	Whitsun

Note, however, that **Noël** (Christmas) is masculine except when used with the definite article: **à la Noël** (at Christmas)

b) *by ending*

-ace	**la place** (square, seat) *But:* **un espace** (space)
-ade	**la salade** (salad) *But:* **le grade** (degree, rank), **le stade** (stadium)
-ance, -anse	**la puissance** (power), **la danse** (dancing)
-ée	**la soirée** (evening), **la journée** (day)

26

	But: **le musée** (museum), **le lycée** (secondary school)
-ence, -ense	**une évidence** (evidence), **la défense** (defence) *But:* **le silence** (silence)
-ère	**la lumière** (light) *But:* **le mystère** (mystery), **le caractère** (character)
-eur	**la peur** (fear) *But:* **le bonheur** (happiness), **le chœur** (choir), **le cœur** (heart), **un honneur** (honour), **le labeur** (toil), **le malheur** (misfortune)
-ie	**la pluie** (rain) *But:* **le génie** (genius), **un incendie** (fire), **le parapluie** (umbrella)
-ière	**la bière** (beer) *But:* **le cimetière** (cemetery)
-oire	**la gloire** (glory) *But:* **le laboratoire** (laboratory), **le pourboire** (tip)
-tion, -sion, -ation, -aison, -ison	
	la fiction (fiction), **la nation** (nation), **la raison** (reason), **la prison** (prison)
-té	**la bonté** (goodness) *But:* **le côté** (side), **le comté** (county), **le traité** (treaty), **le pâté** (pâté)
-tié	**la moitié** (half), **la pitié** (pity)

Most nouns ending in a silent **e** following two consonants are feminine:

la botte (boot), **la couronne** (crown), **la terre** (earth), **la masse** (mass), **la lutte** (struggle)

But: **le verre** (glass), **le parterre** (flower-bed), **le tonnerre** (thunder), **un intervalle** (interval), **le carrosse** (carriage)

3. Difficulties

a) Some nouns may have either gender depending on the sex of the person to whom they refer:

un artiste a (male) artist	**une artiste** a (female) artist
le Russe the Russian (man)	**la Russe** the Russian (woman)

similarly:

un aide/une aide	an assistant
un camarade/une camarade	a friend
un domestique/une domestique	a servant
un enfant/une enfant	a child
un malade/une malade	a patient
un propriétaire/une propriétaire	an owner

b) Others have only one gender for both sexes:

un ange an angel	**un amateur** an amateur	**un auteur** an author
une connaissance an acquaintance	**une dupe** a dupe	**un écrivain** a writer
une personne a person	**le médecin** the doctor	**le peintre** the painter
la recrue the recruit	**le sculpteur** the sculptor (sculptress)	**la sentinelle** the sentry
le témoin the witness	**la victime** the victim	**la vedette** the (film) star

Note, however, that modern French tends to use feminine forms for many different functions. **La ministre**, **la juge** and **la professeur** can now be commonly found in the press, and new forms such as **une écrivaine** have also begun to appear.

c)   The following nouns change meaning according to gender:

	MASCULINE	FEMININE
aide	male assistant	assistance, female assistant
crêpe	mourning band	pancake
critique	critic	criticism
faux	forgery	scythe
livre	book	pound
manche	handle	sleeve
manuvre	labourer	manoeuvre
mémoire	memorandum	memory
mode	method, way	fashion
mort	dead man	death
moule	mould	mussel
page	pageboy	page
pendule	pendulum	clock
physique	physique	physics
poêle	stove	frying pan
poste	post (*job*), set	post office
somme	nap	sum
tour	trick, tour	tower
trompette	trumpeter	trumpet
vapeur	steamer	steam
vase	vase	silt
voile	veil	sail

d)   A few words vary in gender according to their usage. The plural noun **gens** is regarded as feminine when it follows an adjective, and masculine when it precedes it:

de bonnes gens
good people

des gens ennuyeux
boring people

amour, **délice** and **orgue** are masculine when used in the singular and feminine when used in the plural:

un amour de jeunesse
an old flame

des amours malheureuses
unhappy love affairs

un délice inoubliable
an unforgettable delight

des délices infinies
infinite delights

un orgue électrique	**les grandes orgues**
an electric organ	the great organ

e) *City names*

Some city names are traditionally feminine:

La Rochelle	**La Haye**	**Alger la Blanche**
La Rochelle	The Hague	Algiers, the white city

Others are masculine in everyday usage:

le Paris des années 30	**le Londres de mon souvenir**
Paris in the 30s	the London I remember
le vieux Nice	**Berlin fut totalement détruit**
old Nice	Berlin was completely destroyed

In literary French, however, city names are feminine:

Caen fut prise après de terribles bombardements
Caen was taken after a terrible bombardment

B. The Formation Of Feminines

The feminine of nouns may be formed in the following ways:

1. By adding an **e** to the masculine form:

un ami	**une amie**
a (male) friend	a (female) friend
un Hollandais	**une Hollandaise**
a Dutchman	a Dutch woman

Note that nouns which end in **-e** in the masculine form do not change:

un élève	**une élève**
a (male) pupil	a (female) pupil

Note also that the addition of an **e** often entails an alteration of the masculine form:

i) nouns ending in **-t** and **-n** double the final consonant:

le chien	**la chienne** (dog/bitch)
le chat	**la chatte** (cat)

ii) nouns ending in **-er** add a grave accent to the **e** immediately preceding the **r**:

un ouvrier	**une ouvrière** (workman/female worker)

iii) nouns ending in **-eur** change into **-euse**:

le vendeur	**la vendeuse** (male/female shop assistant)

However, a few nouns ending in **-eur** change into **-eresse**:

le pécheur	**la pécheresse** (sinner)

iv) nouns ending in **-teur** change into **-teuse** or **-trice** according to the following guidelines:

if the stem of the word is also that of a present participle the feminine form ends in **-euse**:

le chanteur	**la chanteuse** (male/female singer)

31

NOUNS

if the stem is not that of a present participle, the feminine form ends in **-trice**:

le lecteur   **la lectrice** (male/female reader)

v) nouns ending in **-f** change into **-ve**:

le veuf   **la veuve** (widower/widow)

vi) nouns ending in **-x** change into **-se**:

un époux   **une épouse** (husband/wife)

vii) nouns ending in **-eau** change into **-elle**:

le jumeau   **la jumelle** (male/female twin)

2. By using a different word (as in English):

le beau-fils	**la belle-fille** (son-/daughter-in-law)
le beau-père	**la belle-mère** (father-/mother-in-law)
le bélier	**la brebis** (ram/ewe)
le bœuf	**la vache** (ox/cow)
le canard	**la cane** (drake/duck)
le cheval	**la jument** (horse/mare)
le cerf	**la biche** (stag/hind)
le coq	**la poule** (cock/hen)
le fils	**la fille** (son/daughter)
le frère	**la sœur** (brother/sister)
un homme	**une femme** (man/woman)
un jars	**une oie** (gander/goose)
le mâle	**la femelle** (male/female)
le neveu	**la nièce** (nephew/niece)
un oncle	**une tante** (uncle/aunt)
le parrain	**la marraine** (godfather/godmother)
le père	**la mère** (father/mother)
le porc	**la truie** (pig/sow)
le roi	**la reine** (king/queen)

3. By adding the word **femme** (or **femelle** for animals):

une femme médecin (doctor)
un perroquet femelle (female parrot)

4. Irregular feminine forms

un abbé	une **abbesse** (abbot/abbess)
un âne	une **ânesse** (donkey)
le comte	la **comtesse** (count/countess)
le dieu	la **déesse** (god/goddess)
le duc	la **duchesse** (duke/duchess)
un Esquimau	une **Esquimaude** (Eskimo)
le fou	la **folle** (madman/mad woman)
un Grec	une **Grecque** (Greek)
un héros	une **héroïne** (hero/heroine)
un hôte	une **hôtesse** (host/hostess)
le maître	la **maîtresse** (master/mistress)
le prêtre	la **prêtresse** (priest/priestess)
le prince	la **princesse** (prince/princess)
le tigre	la **tigresse** (tiger/tigress)
le Turc	la **Turque** (Turk)
le vieux	la **vieille** (old man/old woman)

C. The Formation Of Plurals

1. Most nouns form their plural by adding **s** to the singular:

le vin	les vins	wine
un étudiant	des étudiants	student

2. Nouns ending in **-s, -x** or **-z** remain unchanged:

le bras	les bras	arm
la voix	les voix	voice
le nez	les nez	nose

3. Nouns ending in **-au, -eau** and **-eu** add **x** to the singular:

	le tuyau	les tuyaux	drainpipe
	le bateau	les bateaux	boat
	le jeu	les jeux	game
But:	le landau	les landaus	pram
	le bleu	les bleus	bruise
	le pneu	les pneus	tyre

4. Nouns ending in **-al** change to **-aux**:

	le journal	les journaux	newspaper
But:	le bal	les bals	dance
	le carnaval	les carnavals	carnival
	le festival	les festivals	festival

5. Nouns ending in **-ail** change to **-aux**:

	le bail	les baux	lease
	le travail	les travaux	work
	le vitrail	les vitraux	stained-glass window
But:	le détail	les détails	detail
	l'épouvantail	les épouvantails	scarecrow
	l'éventail	les éventails	fan
	le rail	les rails	rail

6. Nouns ending in **-ou**:

a) Seven nouns ending in **-ou** add **x** in the plural:

le bijou	les bijoux	jewel
le caillou	les cailloux	pebble
le chou	les choux	cabbage
le genou	les genoux	knee
le hibou	les hiboux	owl
le joujou	les joujoux	toy
le pou	les poux	louse

b) Other nouns ending in **-ou** add **s**:

le clou	les clous	nail

7. Plural of compound nouns:

Each noun ought to be checked individually in a dictionary:

eg	le chou-fleur	les choux-fleurs	cauliflower
	le beau-père	les beaux-pères	father-in-law
But:	un essuie-glace	des essuie-glaces	windscreen wiper
	le tire-bouchon	les tire-bouchons	corkscrew

8. Irregular plurals:

un œil	des yeux	eye
le ciel	les cieux	sky
Monsieur	Messieurs	Mr
Madame	Mesdames	Mrs
Mademoiselle	Mesdemoiselles	Miss

9. Collective nouns:

a) Some nouns are singular in French but plural in English:

le bétail	cattle
la recette	takings
la police	police

la police *a* arrêté certains grévistes
the police *have* arrested some strikers

b) Others are plural in French but singular in English:

le nouvelles	news
les capitaux	capital
les cheveux	hair

les nouvelles *sont* **bonnes**
the news *is* good

10. Proper nouns:

a) Ordinary family names are invariable:

j'ai rencontré les Leblanc
I met the Leblancs

b) Historical names add **-s**:

les Stuarts	**les Bourbons**	**les Tudors**
the Stuarts	the Bourbons	the Tudors

4. ADJECTIVES

Adjectives usually accompany a noun (or a pronoun) and provide extra information about what someone or something is like:

une *grande* **ville**
a *large* city

un passe-temps *intéressant*
an *interesting* pastime

elle est *espagnole*
she is *Spanish*

c'était *ennuyeux*
it was *boring*

A. Agreement Of Adjectives

In French, adjectives agree in number and gender with the noun or pronoun to which they refer. This means that French adjectives have four different forms which are determined by the noun they accompany:

- ☐ **masculine singular** (basic form, found in the dictionary)
- ☐ **feminine singular**
- ☐ **masculine plural**
- ☐ **feminine plural**

un passeport *vert*
a green passport

une voiture *verte*
a green car

des gants *verts*
green gloves

des chaussettes *vertes*
green socks

Note that if two singular words share the same adjective, the adjective will be in the plural:

un foulard et un bonnet *rouges*
a red scarf and (a red) hat

If one of these words is feminine and the other masculine, the adjective will be in the masculine plural:

une robe et un manteau *noirs*
a black dress and (a black) coat

B. Feminine Forms Of Adjectives

1. General rule

Add the letter **e** to the masculine singular form:

MASCULINE	FEMININE
grand	grande
amusant	amusante
anglais	anglaise
bronzé	bronzée

un livre amusant	une histoire amusante
an amusing book	an amusing story
il est bronzé	elle est bronzée
he is suntanned	she is suntanned

2. Adjectives already ending in -e

These do not change:

MASCULINE	FEMININE
rouge	rouge
jeune	jeune
malade	malade

mon père est malade	ma mère est malade
my father is ill	my mother is ill

3. Others

The spelling of some adjectives changes when the **e** is added:

a) The following masculine endings generally double the final consonant before adding **e**:

MASCULINE ENDING	FEMININE ENDING
-el	-elle
-eil	-eille
-en	-enne
-on	-onne
-as	-asse
-et	-ette

MASCULINE		FEMININE
réel	(real)	réelle
cruel	(cruel)	cruelle
pareil	(similar)	pareille
ancien	(old)	ancienne
italien	(Italian)	italienne
bon	(good)	bonne
gras	(greasy)	grasse
bas	(low)	basse
muet	(dumb)	muette
net	(clear)	nette

un problème actuel a topical problem	**la vie actuelle** present-day life
un bon conseil good advice	**c'est une bonne recette** it's a good recipe

Note, however, that the feminine ending of some common adjectives in **-et** is **-ète** instead of **-ette**:

MASCULINE		FEMININE
complet	(complete)	complète
incomplet	(incomplete)	incomplète
concret	(concrete)	concrète
discret	(discreet)	discrète
inquiet	(worried)	inquiète
secret	(secret)	secrète

b)
MASCULINE IN **-er**		FEMININE IN **-ère**
cher	(dear)	chère
fier	(proud)	fière
dernier	(last)	dernière

c)
MASCULINE IN **-x**		FEMININE IN **-se**
heureux	(happy)	heureuse
malheureux	(unhappy)	malheureuse
sérieux	(serious)	sérieuse
jaloux	(jealous)	jalouse

But:	doux	(soft)	**douce**
	faux	(false)	**fausse**
	roux	(red-haired)	**rousse**
	vieux	(old)	**vieille**

d)

MASCULINE IN -eur		FEMININE IN -euse
menteur	(lying)	menteuse
trompeur	(deceitful)	trompeuse

This rule, however, applies only when the stem of the adjective is also the stem of a present participle (eg **mentant, trompant**). The following five adjectives simply add an **e** to the feminine, **-eur** becoming **-eure**:

MASCULINE		FEMININE
extérieur	(external)	extérieure
intérieur	(internal)	intérieure
inférieur	(inferior)	inférieure
supérieur	(superior)	supérieure
meilleur	(better)	meilleure

The feminine ending of the remaining adjectives in **-teur** is **-trice**:

MASCULINE		FEMININE
protecteur	(protective)	protectrice
destructeur	(destructive)	destructrice

e)

MASCULINE IN -f		FEMININE IN -ve
neuf	(new)	neuve
vif	(lively)	vive
naïf	(naive)	naïve
actif	(active)	active
passif	(passive)	passive
positif	(positive)	positive
bref	(brief)	brève (note the è)

f)

MASCULINE IN -c		FEMININE IN -che or -que
blanc	(white)	blanche
franc	(frank)	franche
sec	(dry)	sèche (note that the e changes to è)
public	(public)	publique
turc	(Turkish)	turque
grec	(Greek)	grecque (note the c)

g) The following five common adjectives have an irregular feminine form and two forms for the masculine singular; the second masculine form, based on the feminine form, is used before words starting with a vowel or a silent **h**:

MASCULINE	FEMININE	MASCULINE 2
beau (beautiful)	belle	bel
nouveau (new)	nouvelle	nouvel
vieux (old)	vieille	vieil
fou (mad)	folle	fol
mou (soft)	molle	mol
un beau lac a beautiful lake	une belle vue a beautiful view	un bel enfant a beautiful child
un nouveau disque a new record	la nouvelle année the new year	un nouvel ami a new friend
un vieux tableau an old painting	la vieille ville the old town	un vieil homme an old man

h) Other irregular feminines:

MASCULINE		FEMININE
favori	(favourite)	favorite
gentil	(nice)	gentille
nul	(no)	nulle

frais	(fresh)	**fraîche**
malin	(shrewd)	**maligne**
sot	(foolish)	**sotte**
long	(long)	**longue**
aigu	(sharp)	**aiguë**
ambigu	(ambiguous)	**ambiguë**
chic	(elegant)	**chic**
châtain	(chestnut)	**châtain**

C. Plurals Of Adjectives

1. General rule

The masculine and feminine plural of adjectives is formed by adding an **s** to the singular form:

un vélo neuf a new bike	des vélos neufs new bikes
une belle fleur a beautiful flower	de belles fleurs beautiful flowers
le livre intéressant the interesting book	les livres intéressants the interesting books

2. Adjectives ending in -s or -x

If the masculine singular ends in **-s** or **-x**, the plural form does not take an **s**:

il est heureux he's happy	ils sont heureux they are happy
un touriste anglais an English tourist	des touristes anglais English tourists

3. Others

A few masculine plurals are irregular (the feminine plurals are all regular):

a)

SINGULAR IN -al		PLURAL IN -aux
normal	(normal)	normaux
brutal	(brutal)	brutaux
loyal	(loyal)	loyaux

But:

fatal	(fatal)	fatals
natal	(native)	natals
naval	(naval)	navals

Note that the adjective **final** (final) has two masculine plural forms: **finals** and **finaux**.

b)

SINGULAR IN **-eau**		PLURAL IN **-eaux**
beau	(beautiful)	**beaux**
nouveau	(new)	**nouveaux**

D. Position Of Adjectives

1. Unlike English adjectives, French adjectives usually follow the noun:

un métier intéressant   **des parents modernes**
an interesting job   modern parents

Adjectives of colour and nationality always follow the noun:

des chaussures rouges   **le drapeau britannique**
red shoes   the British flag

2. However, the following common adjectives generally come before the noun:

beau	beautiful
bon	good
court	short
gentil	nice
grand	big, tall
gros	fat
haut	high
jeune	young
joli	pretty
long	long
mauvais	bad
méchant	nasty, naughty
meilleur	better
moindre	lesser, least
petit	small
pire	worse
vieux	old
vilain	nasty, ugly

3. Some adjectives have a different meaning according to their position:

	BEFORE NOUN	AFTER NOUN
ancien	former	ancient
brave	good	brave
certain	some	sure
cher	dear	expensive

	BEFORE NOUN	AFTER NOUN
dernier	last (*final*)	last (*latest*)
grand	great (*people only*)	big, tall
même	same	very
pauvre	poor (*pitiable*)	poor (*not rich*)
propre	own	clean
seul	single, only	alone, lonely
simple	mere	simple
vrai	real	true

mon ancien métier
my former job

un tableau ancien
an old painting

un brave type
a nice fellow

un homme brave
a brave man

un certain charme
a certain charm

un fait certain
a definite fact

chère Brigitte
dear Brigitte

un cadeau cher
an expensive present

la dernière séance
the last performance

le mois dernier
last month

une grande vedette
a great star

un homme assez grand
a fairly tall man

le même endroit
the same place

la vérité même
the truth itself

mon pauvre ami!
my poor friend!

des gens pauvres
poor people

mon propre frère
my own brother

une chambre propre
a clean room

mon seul espoir
my only hope

un homme seul
a lonely man

un simple employé
an ordinary employee

des goûts simples
simple tastes

un vrai casse-pieds
a real bore

une histoire vraie
a true story

If a noun is accompanied by several adjectives, the same rules apply to each of them:

le bon vieux temps
the good old days

un joli foulard rouge
a pretty red scarf

E. Comparative And Superlative Of Adjectives

Persons or things can be compared by using:

1. *the comparative form of the adjective:*

   more ... than

   ...er than

   less ... than

   not as ... as

   as ... as

2. *the superlative form of the adjective:*

   the most ...

   the ...est

   the least ...

1. The comparative

The French comparative is formed as follows:

plus ... (que) more ... (than) ...er (than)	**plus long** longer	**plus cher** more expensive
moins ... (que) less ... (than) not as ... (as)	**moins long** less long	**moins récent** less recent
aussi ... (que) as ... (as)	**aussi bon** as good	**aussi important** as important

une plus grande maison
a larger house

un village plus ancien
an older village

le football est-il plus populaire que le rugby?
is football more popular than rugby?

ces gants sont moins chauds que les autres
these gloves are less warm than the other ones

elle est beaucoup/bien moins patiente que lui
she's far less patient than he is

> **le problème de la pollution est tout aussi grave**
> the pollution problem is just as serious

2. The superlative

a) *Formation*

le/la/les plus …	the most …, the …est
le/la/les moins …	the least …
le plus grand pays	**la plus grande ville**
the largest country	the largest city
les plus grands acteurs	**les plus grandes voitures**
the greatest actors	the largest cars

b) *Word order*

   i) The normal rules governing word order of adjectives apply. When a superlative adjective comes after the noun, the article is used twice, before the noun and before the adjective:

   le plat le plus délicieux
   the most delicious dish

   l'histoire la plus passionnante
   the most exciting story

   ii) When a possessive adjective is used, there are two possible constructions, depending on the position of the adjective:

   ma plus forte matière
   my best subject

or: **mon besoin le plus urgent est de trouver un emploi**
   my most urgent need is to find a job

c) *'in' is normally translated by **de**:*

   la plus jolie maison du quartier/de la ville
   the prettiest house in the area/town

   le restaurant le plus cher de France
   the most expensive restaurant in France

Note that verbs following the superlative usually take the subjunctive (see p 138).

3. Irregular comparatives and superlatives

ADJECTIVE	COMPARATIVE	SUPERLATIVE
bon	**meilleur**	**le meilleur**
good	better	best
mauvais	**pire**	**le pire**
	plus mauvais	**le plus mauvais**
bad	worse	the worst
petit	**moindre**	**le moindre**
	plus petit	**le plus petit**
small	smaller, lesser	the smallest, the least

Note that **pire** and **le pire** are, strictly speaking, the correct comparative and superlative forms of **mauvais**. **Plus mauvais** and **le plus mauvais** can also be found in everyday French, however, with a slight difference in meaning: **pire** and **le pire** express the absolute (ie one cannot conceive of a worse example of …) while **plus mauvais** and **le plus mauvais** indicate a comparison of a lesser degree:

> **il n'y a pas de pire professeur que lui**
> he is the worst teacher of all

> **c'est la pire chose qui pouvait lui arriver**
> it's the worst thing that could happen to him

> **ma note est plus mauvaise que la tienne**
> my mark is worse than yours

> **c'est le plus mauvais élève de la classe**
> he's the worst pupil in the class

Note, too, that **moindre** usually means 'less in importance', and **plus petit** 'less in size':

> **le moindre de mes soucis**
> the least of my worries

> **elle est plus petite que moi**
> she is smaller than I (am)

F. Adjectives Of Nationality

1. French, unlike English, does not use capital letters for adjectives of
nationality. Only nouns indicating nationality are written with a
capital letter in French:

une voiture anglaise
an English car

une Anglaise
an English woman

2. An adjective of nationality in English is sometimes best translated by a
genitive construction in French:

l'ambassade de France
the French embassy

l'équipe de France de rugby
the French rugby team

l'équipe de Nantes
the Nantes team

l'équipe de Glasgow
the Glasgow *or* Glaswegian
team

le championnat de France
the French league

**le Coupe de France de
football**
the French football cup

la Grand Prix du Brésil
the Brazilian Grand Prix

la terre de France
French soil

la couronne de France
the French crown, the crown
of France

les côtes de France
the French coastline

une grammaire de l'anglais
an English grammar

5. ADVERBS

Adverbs are normally used with a verb to express:

		ADVERBS OF
how		manner
when		time
where	an action is done	place
with how much intensity		intensity
to what extent		quantity

A. Adverbs Of Manner

These are usually formed by adding **-ment** to the adjective (like **-ly** in English):

1. If the adjective ends in a consonant, **-ment** is added to its feminine form:

ADJECTIVE (masc, fem)	ADVERB
doux, douce (soft)	**doucement** (softly)
franc, franche (frank)	**franchement** (frankly)
final, finale (final)	**finalement** (finally)

2. If the adjective ends in a vowel, **-ment** is added to its masculine form:

ADJECTIVE	ADVERB
absolu (absolute)	**absolument** (absolutely)
désespéré (desperate)	**désespérément** (desperately)
vrai (true)	**vraiment** (truly)
simple (simple)	**simplement** (simply)

But:

gai (cheerful)	**gaiement** *or* **gaîment** (cheerfully)
nouveau (new)	**nouvellement** (newly)
fou (mad)	**follement** (madly)

3. Many adverbs have irregular forms:

a) Some change the **e** of the feminine form of the adjective to **é** before adding **-ment**:

ADJECTIVE	ADVERB
commun (common)	**communément** (commonly)
précis (precise)	**précisément** (precisely)
profond (deep)	**profondément** (deeply)
énorme (enormous)	**énormément** (enormously)
aveugle (blind)	**aveuglément** (blindly)

b) Adjectives which end in **-ent** and **-ant** change to **-emment** and **-amment**. Note that both endings are pronounced like **amant**:

ADJECTIVE	ADVERB
prudent (careful)	**prudemment** (carefully)
évident (obvious)	**évidemment** (obviously)
brillant (brilliant)	**brillamment** (brilliantly)

But: **lent** (slow) **lentement** (slowly)

4. Some adverbs are completely irregular, including some of the most commonly used ones:

ADJECTIVE	ADVERB
bon (good)	**bien** (well)
bref (brief)	**brièvement** (briefly)
gentil (kind)	**gentiment** (kindly)
mauvais (bad)	**mal** (badly)
meilleur (better)	**mieux** (better)

5. Some adjectives are also used as adverbs in certain set expressions:

parler bas/haut *or* **fort**	to speak softly/loudly
coûter/payer cher	to cost/pay a lot
s'arrêter net	to stop short
couper court	to cut short
voir clair	to see clearly
marcher droit	to walk straight
travailler dur	to work hard

chanter faux/juste	to sing off key/in tune
sentir mauvais/bon	to smell bad/good
refuser net	to refuse point blank

6. After verbs relating to saying something or looking at something in French an adverbial phrase is often preferred to an adverb:

'tu m'écriras?' dit-il *d'une voix triste*
'will you write to me?' he said *sadly*

elle nous a regardés *d'un air dédaigneux*
she looked at us *disdainfully*

7. English adverbs may be expressed in French by a preposition followed by a noun:

sans soin	carelessly
avec fierté	proudly
avec amour	lovingly

B. Adverbs Of Time

These are not usually formed from adjectives. The commonest ones are
the following:

alors	then
après	afterwards
aujourd'hui	today
aussitôt	at once
bientôt	soon
d'abord	first
déjà	already
demain	tomorrow
encore	still, again
pas encore	not yet
enfin	at last, finally
hier	yesterday
parfois	sometimes
rarement	seldom
souvent	often
tard	late
tôt	early
toujours	always
tout de suite	immediately

c'est déjà Noël!
it's Christmas already!

il mange encore!
he's still eating!

tu as déjà essayé?
have you tried before?

elle n'est pas encore arrivée
she hasn't arrived yet

C. Adverbs Of Place

Like adverbs of time, these are not usually formed from adjectives. The commonest ones are the following:

ailleurs	somewhere else, elsewhere
ici	here
là	there
loin	far away
dessus	on top, on it
au-dessus	over, above
dessous	underneath
au-dessous	below
dedans	inside
dehors	outside
devant	in front, ahead
derrière	behind
partout	everywhere

ne restez pas dehors!
don't stay outside!

qu'est-ce qu'il y a dedans?
what's inside?

mon nom est marqué dessus
my name is written on it

passez devant
go in front

D. Adverbs Of Intensity And Quantity

These may be used with a verb, an adjective or another adverb. The commonest ones are the following:

à peine	hardly
assez	enough, quite
autant	as much/many
beaucoup	a lot, much/many
combien	how much/many
comme	how
moins	less
plus	more
presque	nearly
peu	little
seulement	only
si	so
tant	so much/many
tellement	so much/many
très	very
trop	too, too much/many
un peu	a little

vous avez assez bu!
you've had enough to drink!

il ne fait pas assez chaud
it's not warm enough

nous avons beaucoup ri
we laughed a lot

comme c'est amusant!
how funny!

je vais un peu mieux
I'm feeling a little better

c'est si fatigant!
it's so tiring!

elle parle trop
she talks too much

il est très timide
he's very shy

Note that all of these adverbs, except **à peine**, **comme**, **presque**, **si**, **très** and **seulement**, may be followed by **de** and a noun to express a quantity (see pp 232-3).

E. Position Of Adverbs

1. Adverbs usually follow verbs:

> **je vais rarement au théâtre**
> I seldom go to the theatre

> **comme vous conduisez prudemment**
> you do drive carefully!

2. With compound tenses, shorter adverbs usually come between the auxiliary and the past participle:

> **j'ai enfin terminé**
> I have finished at last

> **nous y sommes souvent allés**
> we've often gone there

> **il me l'a déjà dit**
> he's already told me

> **elle avait beaucoup souffert**
> she had suffered a lot

3. Adverbs of place and many adverbs of time, however, follow the past participle:

> **je l'ai rencontré hier**
> I met him yesterday

> **elle avait cherché partout**
> she had looked everywhere

> **mettez-le dehors**
> put it outside

> **tu t'es couché tard?**
> did you go to bed late?

4. Adverbs usually come before adjectives or other adverbs, as in English:

> **très rarement**
> very seldom

> **trop vite**
> too quickly

> **elle est vraiment belle**
> she is really beautiful

F. Comparative And Superlative Of Adverbs

1. The comparative and superlative of adverbs are formed in the same way as those of adjectives:

ADVERB	COMPARATIVE	SUPERLATIVE
souvent often	**plus souvent (que)** more often (than)	**le plus souvent** (the) most often
	moins souvent (que) less often (than) not as often (as)	**le moins souvent** (the) least often
	aussi souvent (que) as often (as)	

Note that the superlative of the adverb always takes the masculine singular article **le**:

je le vois plus souvent qu'avant
I see him more often than I used to

il conduit moins prudemment que moi
he drives less carefully than I do
he doesn't drive as carefully as I do

c'est lui qui conduit le moins prudemment
he's the one who drives the least carefully

je sais cuisiner aussi bien que toi!
I can cook as well as you!

Note:

a) **as ... as possible** is translated either by **aussi ... que possible** or by **le plus ...possible**:

as far as possible   **aussi loin que possible**
                                le plus loin possible

b) after a negative, **aussi** is often replaced by **si**:

pas si vite!
not so fast!

c) In French, the idea of **not so, not as** is often expressed by **moins** (less):

> **parle moins fort!**
> don't talk so loud!

2. Irregular comparatives and superlatives

ADVERB	COMPARATIVE	SUPERLATIVE
beaucoup much, a lot	**plus** more	**le plus** (the) most
bien well	**mieux** better	**le mieux** (the) best
mal badly	**pis** or **plus mal** worse	**le pis** or **le plus mal** (the) worst
peu little	**moins** less	**le moins** (the) least

> **il est mieux payé que moi**
> he is better paid than me

> **c'est lui le mieux payé**
> he's the best paid

Note:

a) **mieux/le mieux** must not be confused with **meilleur/ le meilleur** which are adjectives, used in front of a noun.

> **elle chante mieux que toi**
> she sings better than you (do)

> **c'est elle qui chante le mieux**
> she sings best

> **elle est meilleure chanteuse que toi**
> she is a better singer than you

> **c'est la meilleure chanteuse**
> she is the best singer

b) **pis/le pis** are only found in certain set expressions or in literary French:

>**tant pis**
>too bad

>**de mal en pis**
>from bad to worse

>**il n'y a rien de pis que cela**
>there is nothing worse than that

>**on en dit pris que pendre**
>nobody has a good word to say about it

6. PRONOUNS AND CORRESPONDING ADJECTIVES

A. Demonstratives

1. Demonstrative adjectives

a) *CE*

ce is often used to point out a particular person or thing, or persons or things. It is followed by the noun to which it refers and agrees in number and gender with that noun:

- □ with a masculine singular noun: **ce (cet)** this/that
- □ with a feminine singular noun: **cette** this/that
- □ with a plural noun (masc or fem): **ces** these/those

ce roman m'a beaucoup plu
I really liked this novel

il a neigé ce matin
it snowed this morning

cette chanson m'énerve
that song gets on my nerves

cette fois, c'est fini!
this time, it's over!

tu trouves que ces lunettes me vont bien?
do you think these glasses suit me?

cet is used instead of **ce** in front of a masculine singular word that begins with a vowel or a silent **h**:

cet été
this summer

cet hôtel
that hotel

b) *-CI* and *-LÀ*

French does not have separate words to distinguish between 'this' and 'that'. However, when a particular emphasis is being placed on a person or object, or when a contrast is being made between persons or objects, **-ci** and **-là** are added to the noun:

-ci translates the idea of this/these
-là translates the idea of that/those

je suis très occupé ces jours-ci
I'm very busy these days

que faisiez-vous ce soir-là?
what were you doing that evening?

tu préfères cette robe-ci ou cette robe-là?
do you prefer this dress or that dress?

2. Demonstrative pronouns

Demonstrative pronouns are used instead of a noun with **ce/cette/ces**. They are:

> celui, celle, ceux, celles
> ce
> ceci, cela, ça

a) CELUI

celui agrees in number and gender with the noun it refers to. It has four different forms:

	MASCULINE	FEMININE
SINGULAR	celui	celle
PLURAL	ceux	celles

celui, celle, ceux and **celles** cannot be used on their own. They are used:

◻ with **-ci** or **-là**, for emphasis or for contrast:

celui-ci	celle-ci	this (one)
celui-là	celle-là	that (one)
ceux-ci	celles-ci	these (ones)
ceux-là	celles-là	those (ones)

j'aime bien ce maillot mais celui-là est moins cher
I like this swimsuit, but that one is cheaper

je voudrais ces fleurs – lesquelles? celles-ci ou celles-là?
I'd like these flowers – which ones? these or those?

◻ with **de** + noun, to express possession:

je préfère mon ordinateur à celui de Jean-Claude
I prefer my computer to Jean-Claude's

range ta chambre plutôt que celle de ta sœur
tidy your own bedroom rather than your sister's

mes parents sont moins sévères que ceux de Nicole
my parents aren't as strict as Nicole's

les douches municipales sont mieux que celles du camping
the public showers are better than those at the campsite

▫ with the relative pronouns **qui, que, dont** to introduce a relative clause (for use of these relative pronouns, see pp 93-9).

celui/celle/ceux/celles qui	the one(s) who/which
celui/celle/ceux/celles que	the one(s) whom/which
celui/celle/ceux/celles dont	the one(s) of which/whose

lequel est ton père? celui qui a une moustache?
which one is your father? the one with the moustache?

regarde cette voiture! celle qui est garée au coin
look at that car! the one which is parked at the corner

deux filles, celles qu'il avait rencontrées la veille
two girls, the ones he had met the day before

voilà mon copain, celui dont je t'ai parlé l'autre jour
here's my friend, the one I told you about the other day

b) CE

ce (meaning 'it' or 'that') is normally used with the verb **être**:

c'est	**ce serait**	**c'était**
it's/that's	it/that would be	it/that was

Note that **ce** changes to **c'** before an **e** or an **é**.

▫ with a noun or pronoun, **ce** is used to identify people or things, or to emphasize them; it is translated in a variety of ways:

qu'est-ce que c'est? – c'est mon billet d'avion
what's that? – it's my plane ticket

qui est-ce? – c'est moi | **ce doit être lui**
who is it? – it's me | that must be him

c'est un artiste bien connu | **c'était une bonne idée**
he's a well-known artist | it was a good idea

ce sont mes amis	**c'est la dernière fois!**
they're my friends	it's the last time!
c'est elle qui l'a fait	**c'est celui que j'ai vu**
she's the one who did it	he's the one I saw
ce sont des gens sympathiques	**ce ne sont pas mes chaussures**
they're nice people	those aren't my shoes

□ before an adjective, **ce** is used to refer to an idea, an event or a fact which has already been mentioned; it does not refer to any specific noun:

c'était formidable	**ce serait amusant**
it was great	it would be funny
oui, c'est vrai	**c'est sûr?**
yes, that's true	is that definite?
ce n'est pas grave	**c'est bon à entendre**
it doesn't matter or it's not serious	that's good to hear
c'est exact!	**c'est rare qu'il pleuve en juin**
that's right!	it doesn't often rain in June

Note that the translation of **it** is an area of some difficulty for students of French, as it is sometimes translated by **ce** and sometimes by **il/elle**; see pp 258-9 for further information.

c) *CECI, CELA, ÇA*

ceci (this), **cela** (that) and **ça** (that) are used to refer to an idea, an event, a fact or an object. They never refer to a particular noun already mentioned.

non, je n'aime pas ça!	**ah, bon? cela m'étonne**
no, I don't like that!	really? that surprises me
ça, c'est un acteur!	**souvenez-vous de ceci**
that's what I call an actor!	remember this
ça m'est égal	**cela ne vous regarde pas**
I don't mind	that's none of your business
buvez ceci, ça vous fera du bien	
drink this, it'll do you good	

ça alors!
well, really!

cela s'appelle comment, en anglais?
what do you call this in English?

Note that **ceci** is not very common in French; **cela** and **ça** are often used to translate 'this' as well as 'that'; **ça** is used far more frequently than **cela** in spoken French.

B. Indefinite Adjectives And Pronouns

1. Indefinite adjectives

They are:

MASCULINE	FEMININE	
autre(s)	autre(s)	other
certain(s)	certaine(s)	certain
chaque	chaque	each, every
même(s)	même(s)	same
plusieurs	plusieurs	several
quelque(s)	quelque(s)	some
tel(s)	telle(s)	such
tout (tous)	toute(s)	all, every

Note that, when used as indefinite adjectives, all the above adjectives are placed before the nouns to which they refer. **Certain** and **même** can be found after the noun but they will then have a different meaning (see pp 45-6).

a) *CHAQUE and PLUSIEURS*

chaque (each) is always singular, **plusieurs** (several) always plural; the feminine form is the same as the masculine form:

j'y vais chaque jour	**chaque personne**
I go there every day	each person
plusieurs années	**il a plusieurs amis**
several years	he's got several friends

b) *AUTRE, MÊME and QUELQUE*

autre (other), **même** (same) and **quelque** (some) agree in number with the noun that follows; the feminine is the same as the masculine:

je voudrais un autre café	**d'autres couleurs**
I'd like another coffee	other colours
la même taille	**les mêmes touristes**
the same size	the same tourists

quelque temps après some time later	**à quelques kilomètres** a few kilometres away

c) *CERTAIN, TEL and TOUT*

certain (certain, some), **tel** (such) and **tout** (all) agree in number and gender with the noun; they have four different forms:

un certain charme a certain charm	**une certaine dame** a certain lady
à certains moments at (certain) times	**certaines personnes** some people
un tel homme such a man	**une telle aventure** such an adventure
de tels avantages such advantages	**de telles difficultés** such difficulties

quoi! tu as mangé tout le fromage et tous les fruits?
what! you've eaten all the cheese and all the fruit?

toute la journée all day long	**toutes mes matières** all my subjects

Note:

i) **tel**: the position of the article **un/une** with **tel** is not the same as in English: **un tel homme** = such a man.

ii) **tel** cannot qualify another adjective; when it is used as an adverb, 'such' is translated by **si** or **tellement**:

c'était un si bon repas/un repas tellement bon!
it was such a good meal!

iii) **tous les/toutes les** are often translated by 'every':

tous les jours every day	**toutes les places** all seats, every seat

2. Indefinite pronouns

a) These are:

MASCULINE	FEMININE	
aucun	aucune	none, not any
autre(s)	autre(s)	another one, other ones
certains	certaine(s)	certain, some
chacun	chacune	each one, every one
on		everyone, one, someone, you, they, people, we
personne		nobody
plusieurs	plusieurs	several (ones)
quelque chose		something, anything
quelqu'un		someone
quelques-uns	quelques-unes	some, a few
rien		nothing
tout (tous)	toute(s)	everything, every one, all

pas celui-là, l'autre
not that one, the other one

où sont les autres?
where are the others?

certains disent que …
some say that …

personne n'est venu
no one came

qui est là? – personne
who's there? – nobody

qu'as-tu? – rien
what's wrong? – nothing

plusieurs d'entre eux
several of them

chacun pour soi!
every man for himself!

il manque quelque chose?
is anything missing?

dis quelque chose!
say something!

quelqu'un l'a averti
someone warned him

il y a quelqu'un?
is anyone in?

j'ai tout oublié
I've forgotten everything

c'est tout, merci
that's all, thanks

elles sont toutes arrivées
they've all arrived

allons-y tous ensemble
let's all go together

PRONOUNS

b) *Points to note*

i) **aucun(e), personne** and **rien**: these can be used on their own, but they are more often used with a verb and the negative word **ne** (see negative expressions, pp 245-8):

personne n'habite ici
no one lives here

il n'y a rien à manger
there's nothing to eat

ii) **aucun(e), un(e) autre, d'autres, certain(e)s, plusieurs** and **quelques-un(e)s**: when these pronouns are used as direct objects, the pronoun **en** must be used before the verb:

je n'en ai lu aucun
I haven't read any (of them)

donne-m'en une autre
give me another one

j'en ai vu d'autres qui étaient moins chers
I saw other ones which were cheaper

j'en connais certains
I know some of them

il y en a plusieurs
there are several

tu m'en donnes quelques-uns?
will you give me a few?

achètes-en quelques-unes
buy a few

iii) **personne, quelque chose, rien, plusieurs**: when these are followed by an adjective, the preposition **de** (or **d'**) must be used in front of the adjective:

il n'y a personne de libre
there's no one available

quelque chose de mieux
something better

il y en avait plusieurs de cassés
several of them were broken

rien de grave
nothing serious

iv) **autre** is commonly used in the following expressions:

quelqu'un d'autre

someone else

**quelque chose
d'autre**

something else

rien d'autre

nothing else

c) *ON*

This pronoun is used in a variety of ways in French. It can mean:

i) *one/you/they/people* in a general sense:

> **en France, on roule à droite**
> in France, they drive on the right

> **on ne sait jamais**
> you/one never know(s)

> **on ne doit pas mentir**
> you shouldn't lie

ii) *someone* (an undefined person)

In this sense, **on** is often translated by the passive (see p 161):

> **on me l'a déjà dit**
> someone's already told me
> I've already been told

> **on vous l'apportera**
> someone will bring it to you
> it will be brought to you

iii) *we*

In spoken French, **on** is frequently used instead of **nous**; although it refers to a plural subject, it is followed by the third person singular:

> **qu'est-ce qu'on fait?**
> what shall we do?

> **fais vite, on t'attend!**
> hurry up, we're waiting for
> you!

Note that in compound tenses with the auxiliary **être**, the agreement of the past participle with **on** is optional:

> **on est allé au cinéma**
> **on est allés au cinéma**
> we went to the cinema

> **on est rentré en taxi**
> **on est rentrées en taxi**
> we went home by taxi

C. Interrogative And Exclamatory Adjectives And Pronouns

1. The interrogative adjective QUEL?

a) *Forms*

quel (which, what) agrees in number and gender with the noun it refers to. It has four forms:

- with a masculine singular noun: **quel?**
- with a feminine singular noun: **quelle?**
- with a masculine plural noun: **quels?**
- with a feminine plural noun: **quelles?**

b) *Direct questions:*

quel est votre passe-temps favori?
what's your favourite pastime?

quelle heure est-il?
what time is it?

quels jours as-tu de libres?
which days have you got free?

quelles affaires comptes-tu prendre avec toi?
what/which things do you intend to take with you?

c) *Indirect questions:*

je ne sais pas quel CD choisir
I don't know which CD to choose

il se demande quelle veste lui va le mieux
he's wondering which jacket suits him best

2. The exclamatory adjective QUEL!

quel! has the same forms as the interrogative adjective **quel?**:

quel dommage!
what a pity!

quelle belle maison!
what a beautiful house!

quels imbéciles!
what idiots!

quelles jolies chaussures!
what lovely shoes!

3. Interrogative pronouns

These are:

lequel/laquelle/ lesquels/lesquelles?	which (one(s))?
qui?	who?/whom?
que?	what?
quoi?	what?
ce qui	what
ce que	what

ce qui and **ce que** are used only in indirect questions; all other interrogative pronouns can be used both in direct and indirect questions.

a) *LEQUEL?*

i) forms

lequel (which?, which one?) agrees in gender and in number with the noun it stands for:

□ with a masculine singular noun:	**lequel?**	which (one)?
□ with a feminine singular noun:	**laquelle?**	which (one)?
□ with a masculine plural noun:	**lesquels?**	which (ones)?
□ with a feminine plural noun:	**lesquelles?**	which (ones)?

After the prepositions **à** and **de**, the following changes occur:

à + lequel?	→	auquel?
à + lesquels?	→	auxquels?
à + lesquelles?	→	auxquelles?
de + lequel?	→	duquel?
de + lesquels?	→	desquels?
de + lesquelles?	→	desquelles?

Note that **à/de + laquelle?** do not contract.

ii) direct questions:

je cherche un hôtel; lequel recommandez-vous?
I'm looking for a hotel; which one do you recommend?

nous avons plusieurs couleurs; vous préférez laquelle?
we have several colours; which one do you prefer?

lesquels de ces livres sont à toi?
which of these books are yours?

je voudrais essayer ces chaussures – lesquelles?
I would like to try these shoes on – which ones?

iii) indirect questions:

demande-lui lequel de ces ordinateurs est le moins cher
ask him/her which (one) of these computers is the cheapest

c'est dans une de ces rues mais je ne sais plus laquelle
it's in one of these streets, but I can't remember which one

b) QUI?

qui (who?, whom?) is used to refer to people; it can be both subject and object and can be used after a preposition:

qui t'a accompagné? who came/went with you?	**qui as-tu appelé?** who did you call?
tu y vas avec qui? who are you going with?	**c'est pour qui?** who is it for?
pour qui vous prenez-vous? who do you think you are?	**à qui l'as-tu donné?** who did you give it to?

Note that **qui** does **not** contract to **qu'** before a vowel or a silent **h**:

qui est-ce qu'elle attend?
who is she waiting for?

qui? can be replaced by **qui est-ce qui?** (subject) or **qui est-ce que?** (object) in direct questions:

qui est-ce qui veut du café? who wants coffee?	**qui est-ce que tu as vu?** who did you see?

avec qui est-ce que tu sors ce soir?
who are you going out with tonight?

Note, however, that **qui** cannot be replaced by **qui est-ce qui** or **qui est-ce que** in indirect questions:

> **j'aimerais savoir qui vous a dit ça**
> I'd like to know who told you that

> **elle se demandait de qui étaient les fleurs**
> she was wondering who the flowers were from

For more details on the use of **qui/que** as relative pronouns, see pp 93-9.

c) QUE?

que (what?) is used to refer to things. It is only used in direct questions, is always a direct object and cannot be used after prepositions:

> **que désirez-vous?**   **qu'a-t-il dit?**
> what do you wish?   what did he say?

que? is rather formal and is usually replaced by **qu'est-ce qui?** or **qu'est-ce que?** in spoken French.

Note that **que** becomes **qu'** before a vowel or a silent **h**.

d) QU'EST-CE QUI?

qu'est-ce qui? (what?) is used as the subject of a verb; it cannot refer to a person:

> **qu'est-ce qui t'est arrivé?**
> what happened to you?

> **qu'est-ce qui la fait rire?**
> what makes her laugh?

e) QU'EST-CE QUE?

qu'est-ce que? (what?) replaces **que?** as the object of a verb; it becomes **qu'est-ce qu'** before a vowel or a silent **h**:

> **qu'est-ce que tu aimes lire?**
> what do you like reading?

> **qu'est-ce qu'il va faire pendant les vacances?**
> what's he going to do during the holidays?

f) QUOI?

quoi? (what?) refers to things; it is used:

i) instead of **que** or **qu'est-ce que** after a preposition:

à quoi penses-tu?
what are you thinking about?

dans quoi l'as-tu mis?
what did you put it in?

ii) in indirect questions:

demandez-lui de quoi il a besoin
ask him what he needs

je ne sais pas à quoi ça sert
I don't know what it's for

g) CE QUI, CE QUE

ce qui and **ce que** (what) are only used in indirect questions; they replace **qu'est-ce qui** and **(qu'est-ce) que**.

They are used in the same way as the relative pronouns **ce qui** and **ce que** (see pp 97-9).

i) **ce qui** is used as the subject of the verb in the indirect question (**ce qui** is the subject of **s'est passé** in the following example):

nous ne saurons jamais ce qui s'est passé
we'll never know what happened

ii) **ce que** (**ce qu'** before a vowel or a silent **h**) is used as the object of the verb in the indirect question (**ce que** is the object of **il faisait** in the following example):

je n'ai pas remarqué ce qu'il faisait
I didn't notice what he was doing

D. Personal Pronouns

There are four categories of personal pronouns:

- **subject** pronouns
- **object** pronouns
- **disjunctive** pronouns
- **reflexive** pronouns

For reflexive pronouns, see pp 118-9.

1. Subject pronouns

PERSON	SINGULAR		PLURAL	
1st	**je (j')**	I	**nous**	we
2nd	**tu**	you	**vous**	you
3rd	**il**	he, it	**ils**	they
	elle	she, it	**elles**	they
	on	one, we, they		

Note:

a) **je** changes to **j'** before a vowel or a silent **h**:

j'ai honte	**j'adore les frites**
I'm ashamed	I love chips
j'habite en Écosse	
I live in Scotland	

b) **tu** and **vous**

vous can be plural or singular; it is used when speaking to more than one person (plural), or to a stranger or an older person (singular):

vous venez, les gars?	**pourriez-vous m'indiquer**
are you coming, guys?	**la gare?**
	could you show me the way
	to the station?

tu is used when speaking to a friend, a relative, a younger person, or someone else you know well:

tu viens, Marc?
are you coming, Marc?

c) **il/ils, elle/elles** may refer to people, animals or things, and must be of the same gender as the noun they replace:

ton stylo? *il* **est là**
your pen? there *it* is

ta montre? *elle* **est là**
your watch? there *it* is

tes gants? *ils* **sont là**
your gloves? there *they* are

tes lunettes? *elles* **sont là**
your glasses? there *they* are

When referring to several nouns of different genders, French uses the masculine plural **ils**:

> **j'ai trouvé dans mon sac** *un* **stylo et** *une* **montre.** *Ils* **ne m'appartiennent pas**
> I found a pen and a watch in my bag. *They* don't belong to me

d) **on**: see p 71.

2. Object pronouns

There are three types of object pronouns:

- ◻ direct object pronouns
- ◻ indirect object pronouns
- ◻ the pronouns **en** and **y**

a) *Forms*

	PERSON	DIRECT	INDIRECT
SING	1st	**me (m')** me	**me (m')** (to) me
	2nd	**te (t')** you	**te (t')** (to) you
	3rd	**le (l')** him, it	**lui** (to) him
		la (l') her, it	**lui** (to) her
PLUR	1st	**nous** us	**nous** (to) us
	2nd	**vous** you	**vous** (to) you
	3rd	**les** them	**leur** (to) them

Note:

i) **me, te, le** and **la** change to **m', t'** and **l'** before a vowel or a silent **h**:

il m'énerve!
he gets on my nerves!

je m'habituerai à lui
I'll get used to him

ii) **te** and **vous**: the same distinction should be made as between the subject pronouns **tu** and **vous** (see p 77).

iii) **le** is sometimes used in an impersonal sense to refer to a fact, a statement or an idea which has already been expressed; it is usually not translated in English:

j'irai aux États-Unis un jour; en tout cas je *l*'espère
I'll go to the States one day; I hope so anyway

elle a eu un bébé – je *le* sais, elle me *l*'a dit
she's had a baby – I know, she told me

iv) when used as an indirect object pronoun, **lui** can be masculine or feminine:

pose-lui la question
ask him/her the question

j'ai décidé de lui offrir un cadeau
I've decided to give him/her a present

v) when they are used with imperatives, **moi** and **toi** are used instead of **me** and **te**, except when **en** follows:

écris-*moi* bientôt
write to me soon

donne *m*'en
give me some

b) *Position*

In French, object pronouns come immediately before the verb they refer to. With a compound tense, they come before the auxiliary:

on *t*'attendra ici
we'll wait for you here

je *l*'ai rencontrée en ville
I met her in town

Note that when there are two verbs, the pronoun comes immediately before the verb to which it refers:

j'aimerais lui demander
I'd like to ask him/her

tu l'as entendu chanter?
have you heard him sing?

In positive commands (the affirmative imperative) the pronoun follows the verb and is joined to it by a hyphen:

regarde-*les*!
look at them!

parle-*lui*!
speak to him/her!

dis-*nous* ce qui s'est passé
tell us what happened

c) *Direct pronouns and indirect pronouns*

i) Direct object pronouns replace a noun which directly follows the verb. They answer the question 'who(m)?' or 'what?'

WHO(M) did you see?
qui as-tu vu?

I saw *my friend*; I saw *him*
j'ai vu *mon ami*; je *l*'ai vu

tu *me* connais
you know *me*

j'aime *le* voir danser
I like to see *him* dance

je *les* ai trouvés
I found *them*

ne *nous* ennuie pas!
don't bother *us*!

ii) Indirect object pronouns replace a noun which follows the verb with a linking preposition (usually **à**, to whom?). They answer the question 'who to?'

WHO did you speak to?
à qui as-tu parlé?

I spoke *to Marc*; I spoke *to him*
j'ai parlé *à Marc*; je *lui* ai parlé

elle *lui* a menti
she lied *to him/her*

je *te* donne ce CD
I'm giving this CD *to you*

je ne *leur* parle plus
I'm not talking *to them* any more

iii) **le/la/les** or **lui/leur**?

Direct pronouns differ from indirect pronouns only in the 3rd person and great care must be taken to use the correct one:

□ English indirect object pronouns often look like direct objects; this becomes obvious when the object is placed at the end of the clause, after a linking preposition:

I showed him your photo   =   I showed your photo to him
                                  je *lui* ai montré ta photo

This is particularly the case with the following verbs:

acheter	to buy	**offrir**	to offer, to give
donner	to give	**prêter**	to lend
montrer	to show	**vendre**	to sell

je *lui* ai acheté un livre
I bought him/her a book
= I bought a book *for him/her*

ne *leur* prête pas mes affaires
don't lend them my things
= don't lend my things *to them*

□ Some verbs take a direct object in English and an indirect object in French (see p 204):

je ne *lui* ai rien dit
I didn't tell *him/her* anything

je *leur* demanderai
I'll ask *them*

tu *lui* ressembles
you look like *him/her*

téléphone-*leur*
phone *them*

□ Some verbs take a direct object in French and an indirect object in English (see p 203):

je *l'*attends
I'm waiting for *him/her*

écoutez-*les*!
listen *to them*!

d) *Order of object pronouns*

When several object pronouns are used together, they come in the following order:

i) Before the verb:

1	me	te		nous		vous	
2		le	la		les		
3			lui		leur		

il *me l'*a donné
he gave it to me

je vais *vous les* envoyer
I'll send them to you

ne *la leur* vends pas
don't sell it to them

je *le lui* ai acheté
I bought it for him/her

ii) After the verb:

With a positive command (the affirmative imperative), the order is as follows:

1		le	la		les
2	moi (m')	toi (t')		nous	vous
3		lui	leur		

apporte-*les-moi*!
bring them to me!

dites-*le-lui*!
tell him/her!

prête-*la-nous*!
lend it to us!

rends-*la-leur*!
give it back to them!

3. The pronoun EN

a) *Use*

en is used instead of **de** + noun. Since **de** has a variety of meanings, en can be used in a number of ways:

i) It means 'of it/them', but also 'with it/them', 'about it/them', 'from it/there', 'out of it/there':

tu es sûr *du prix*? – j'*en* suis sûr
are you sure of the price? – I'm sure *of it*

je suis content *de ce cadeau*; j'*en* suis content
I'm pleased with this present; I'm pleased *with it*

elle est folle *des animaux*; elle *en* est folle
she's crazy about animals; she's crazy *about them*

il est descendu *du train*; il *en* est descendu
he got off the train; he got *off it*

il revient *de Paris*; il *en* revient
he's coming back from Paris; he's coming back *from there*

ii) Verbal constructions

Particular care should be taken with verbs and expressions which are followed by **de** + noun. Since **de** is not always translated in the same way, **en** may have a number of meanings:

il a envie *de ce livre*; il *en* a envie
he wants this book; he wants *it*

je te remercie *de ton aide*; je t'*en* remercie
thank you for your help; thank you *for it*

tu as besoin *de ces papiers*? tu *en* as besoin?
do you need these papers? do you need *them*?

elle a peur *des chiens*; elle *en* a peur
she's afraid of dogs; she's afraid *of them*

tu te souviens *de ce film*? tu t'*en* souviens?
do you remember this film? do you remember *it*?

iii) 'some'/'any'

en replaces the partitive article (**du, de la, des**) + noun; it means 'some'/'any':

tu veux *du café*? – non, je n'*en* veux pas
do you want (any) coffee? – no, I don't want *any*

j'achète *des fruits*? – non, j'*en* ai chez moi
shall I buy (some) fruit? – no, I've got *some* at home

il y a *de la place*? – *en* voilà là-bas
is there any room? – there's some over there

iv) Expressions of quantity

en must be used with expressions of quantity not followed by a noun. It replaces **de** + noun and means 'of it/them', but is seldom translated in English:

tu as pris assez *d'argent*? tu *en* as pris assez?
did you take enough money? did you take enough?

vous avez *combien de frères*? – j'*en* ai deux
how many brothers do you have? – I've got two

j'ai fini *mes cigarettes*; je vais *en* acheter un paquet
I've finished my cigarettes; I'm going to buy a packet

b) *Position*

Like object pronouns, **en** comes immediately before the verb, except with positive commands (the affirmative imperative), where it comes after the verb and is linked to it by a hyphen:

j'*en* veux un kilo
I want a kilo (of it/them)

prends-*en* assez!
take enough (of it/them)!

j'*en* ai marre!
I'm fed up (with it)!

laisses-*en* aux autres!
leave some for the others!

When used in conjunction with other object pronouns, it always comes last:

ne *m'en* parlez pas!
don't tell me about it!

je *vous en* donnerai
I'll give you some

prête-*lui-en*!
lend him/her some!

gardez-*nous-en*!
keep some for us!

4. The pronoun Y

a) *Use*

y is used instead of **à** + noun, but never refers to a person. It is used:

i) As the indirect object of a verb. Since the preposition **à** is translated in a variety of ways in English, **y** may have various meanings (it, of it/them, about it/them etc):

tu joues *au tennis*? – non, j'*y* joue rarement
do you play tennis? – no, I seldom play (*it*)

je pense *à mon pays natal*; j'*y* pense souvent
I'm thinking *about* my home country; I often think *about it*

il s'intéresse *à la photo*; il s'*y* intéresse
he's interested in photography; he's interested *in it*

ii) To mean 'there':

j'ai passé deux jours *à Londres*; j'*y* ai passé deux jours
I spent two days in London; I spent two days there

il est allé *en Grèce*; il *y* est allé
he went to Greece; he went there

Note that **y** must always be used with the verb **aller** (to go) when the place is not mentioned in the clause. It is often not translated in English:

comment vas-tu *à l'école*? – j'*y* vais en bus
how do you get to school? – I go (there) by bus

allons-*y*!   **on *y* va demain**
let's go!   we're going (there) tomorrow

iii) To replace the prepositions **en, dans, sur** + noun; **y** then means 'there', 'in it/them', 'on it/them':

je voudrais vivre *en France*; je voudrais *y* vivre
I'd like to live in France; I'd like to live *there*

je les ai mis *dans ma poche*; je les *y* ai mis
I put them in my pocket; I put them *there*

sur la table? non, je ne l'*y* vois pas
on the table? no, I don't see it *there*

b) *Position*

Like other object pronouns, **y** comes immediately before the verb,
except with a positive command (the affirmative imperative), where it
must follow the verb:

j'*y* réfléchirai
I'll think about it

il s'*y* est habitué
he got used to it

pensez-*y*!
think about it!

n'*y* allez pas!
don't go!

When used with other object pronouns, **y** comes last:

il va *nous y* rencontrer
he'll meet us there

je l'*y* ai vu hier
I saw him there yesterday

5. Disjunctive pronouns

a) *Forms*

PERSON	SINGULAR	PLURAL
1st	**moi**	**nous**
	me	us
2nd	**toi**	**vous**
	you	you
3rd (masculine)	**lui**	**eux**
	him	them
(feminine)	**elle**	**elles**
	her	them
(impersonal)	**soi**	
	oneself	

Note:

    i) **toi/vous**: the same difference should be made as between **tu** and **vous** (see p 77).

    ii) **soi** is used in an impersonal, general sense to refer to indefinite pronouns and adjectives (**on, chacun, tout le monde, personne, chaque** etc); it is mainly found in set phrases, such as:

        chacun pour soi
        every man for himself

        cela va de soi
        that goes without saying

b) *Use*

Disjunctive pronouns, also called emphatic pronouns, are used instead of object pronouns when referring to persons in the following cases:

i) In answer to a question, alone or in a phrase without a verb:

    qui est là? – moi   **j'ai aimé ce film; et toi?**
    who's there? – me   I liked that film; did you?

    qui préfères-tu, lui ou elle? – elle, bien sûr
    who do you prefer, him or her? – her, of course

ii) After **c'est/ce sont, c'était/c'étaient** etc:

    ouvrez, c'est moi!   **non, ce n'était pas lui**
    open up, it's me!   no, it wasn't him

iii) After a preposition:

    vous allez chez lui?   **tu y vas avec elle?**
    are you going to his place?   are you going with her?

    regarde devant toi!   **oh, c'est pour moi?**
    look in front of you!   oh, is that for me?

iv) With verbal constructions. Special care should be taken when the verb is followed by a preposition:

    tu peux compter sur moi   **quoi! tu as peur de lui?**
    you can count on me   what! you're afraid of him?

il m'a parlé de toi
he told me about you

je pense souvent à vous
I often think about you

Note that emphatic pronouns are only used when referring to people.
In other cases **y** or **en** must be used.

v) For emphasis, particularly when two pronouns are contrasted. The
unstressed subject pronoun is usually included:

vous, vous m'énervez!
you get on my nerves!

lui, il joue bien; elle, non
he plays well; *she* doesn't

moi, je n'aime pas l'hiver
I don't like winter

eux, ils sont partis
they've left

vi) In the case of multiple subjects (two pronouns or one pronoun and
one noun):

lui et son frère sont dans l'équipe
he and his brother are in the team

ma famille et moi allons très bien
my family and I are very well

vii) As the second element of a comparison:

il est plus sympa que toi
he is nicer than you

elle chante mieux que lui
she sings better than he does

viii) Before a relative pronoun:

c'est lui que j'aime
he's the one I love

c'est toi qui l'as dit
you're the one who said it

lui qui n'aime pas le vin blanc en a bu six verres
he who doesn't like white wine had six glasses

ix) With **-même(s)** (-self, -selves), **aussi** (too), **seul** (alone):

faites-le vous-mêmes
do it yourselves

j'irai moi-même
I'll go myself

lui aussi est parti
he too went away

elle seule le sait
she alone knows

x) To replace a possessive pronoun (see p 91-2):

c'est le mien; il est à moi
it's mine; it belongs to me

cette valise n'est pas à lui?
doesn't that suitcase belong to him?

E. Possessive Adjectives And Pronouns

1. Possessive adjectives

a) *Forms*

Possessive adjectives always come before their related noun. Like other adjectives, they agree in gender and number with the noun; the masculine and feminine plural forms are identical:

SINGULAR		PLURAL	
MASC	FEM	(MASC AND FEM)	
mon	ma	mes	my
ton	ta	tes	your
son	sa	ses	his/her/its/one's
notre	notre	nos	our
votre	votre	vos	your
leur	leur	leurs	their

j'ai mis mon argent et mes affaires dans mon sac
I've put my money and my things in my bag

comment va ton frère? et ta sœur? et tes parents?
how's your brother? and your sister? and your parents?

notre rue est assez calme   **ce sont vos amis**
our street is fairly quiet   they're your friends

Note that **mon/ton/son** are used instead of **ma/ta/sa** when the next word starts with a vowel or silent **h**:

mon ancienne maison   **ton amie Christine**
my old house   your friend Christine

son haleine sentait l'alcool
his/her breath smelled of alcohol

b) *Use*

i) The possessive adjective is repeated before each noun and agrees in number and gender with it:

mon père et ma mère sont sortis
my mother and father have gone out

ii) son/sa/ses

son, **sa** and **ses** can all mean 'his', 'her' or 'its'. In French, the form of the adjective is determined by the gender and number of the noun that follows, and not by the possessor:

> **il m'a prêté sa mobylette et son casque**
> he lent me his moped and his helmet

> **elle s'entend bien avec sa mère mais pas avec son père**
> she gets on well with her mother, but not with her father

> **elle vit pour son travail; lui pour ses enfants**
> she lives for her job; he lives for his children

iii) ton/ta/tes and votre/vos

The two sets of words for 'your', **ton/ta/tes** and **votre/vos**, correspond to the two different forms of **tu** and **vous**; they must not be used together with the same person:

> **tu as parlé à ton patron?**
> have you spoken to your boss?

> **Monsieur, vous oubliez votre parapluie!**
> excuse me, sir, you've forgotten your umbrella!

iv) In French, the possessive adjective is replaced by the definite article (**le/la/les**) with the following:

□ parts of the body:

> **il s'est essuyé les mains**   **elle a haussé les épaules**
> he wiped his hands   she shrugged (her shoulders)

□ descriptive phrases at the end of a clause, where English adds 'with':

> **il marchait lentement, les mains dans les poches**
> he was walking slowly, with his hands in his pockets

> **elle l'a regardé partir, les larmes aux yeux**
> she watched him leave with tears in her eyes

2. Possessive pronouns

SINGULAR MASC	FEM	PLURAL (MASC AND FEM)	
le mien	la mienne	les mien(ne)s	mine
le tien	la tienne	les tien(ne)s	yours
le sien	la sienne	les sien(ne)s	his/hers/its
le nôtre	la nôtre	les nôtres	ours
le vôtre	la vôtre	les vôtres	yours
le leur	la leur	les leurs	theirs

Possessive pronouns are used instead of a possessive adjective + noun. They agree in gender and in number with the noun they stand for, and not with the possessor (it is particularly important to remember this when translating 'his' and 'hers'):

j'aime bien ton appartement mais je préfère le mien
I quite like your flat, but I prefer mine

on prend quelle voiture? la mienne ou la tienne?
which car shall we take? mine or yours?

comment sont vos profs? les nôtres sont sympas
what are your teachers like? ours are nice

j'avais mon passeport mais Brigitte avait oublié le sien
I had my passport, but Brigitte had forgotten hers

j'ai gardé ma moto mais Paul a vendu la sienne
I've kept my motorbike but Paul has sold his

à or de + possessive pronoun

The prepositions **à** and **de** combine with the articles **le** and **les** in the usual way:

à + le mien	→	au mien
à + les miens	→	aux miens
à + les miennes	→	aux miennes
de + le mien	→	du mien
de + les miens	→	des miens
de + les miennes	→	des miennes

demande à tes parents, j'ai déjà parlé aux miens
ask your parents, I've already spoken to mine

leur appartement ressemble beaucoup au nôtre
their flat is very similar to ours

j'aime bien les chiens mais j'ai peur du tien
I like dogs, but I'm afraid of yours

Note that after the verb **être**, the possessive pronoun is often replaced by **à** + emphatic pronoun (see p 88):

à qui est cette écharpe? – elle est à moi
whose scarf is this? – it's mine

ce livre est à toi? – non, il est à elle
is this book yours? – no, it's hers

c'est à qui? à vous ou à lui?
whose is this? yours or his?

F. Relative Pronouns

1. Definition

Relative pronouns are words which introduce a relative clause. In the sentence:

I bought the book which you recommended

'which' is the relative pronoun, 'which you recommended' is the relative clause and 'the book' is the antecedent (ie the noun to which the relative pronoun refers).

2. Forms

Relative pronouns are:

qui	who/which	lequel	which
que	who(m)/which	dont	of which/whose
quoi	what	ce qui	what
où	where	ce que	what

qui, que, quoi, lequel, ce qui and ce que can also be used as interrogative pronouns (see pp 73-6) and must not be confused with them.

3. Use

a) *QUI*

qui is used as the subject of a relative clause. It means:

i) 'who', 'that' (referring to people):

est-ce que tu connais le monsieur qui habite ici?
do you know the man who lives here?

ce n'est pas lui qui a menti
he's not the one who lied

ii) 'which', 'that' (referring to things):

tu as pris le journal qui était sur la télé?
did you take the paper which/that was on the TV?

PRONOUNS

b) *QUE*

que (which contracts to **qu'** before a vowel or a silent **h**) is used as the object of a relative clause; it is often not translated. It means:

i) 'who(m)', 'that' (referring to people):

la fille que j'aime ne m'aime pas
the girl (that) I love doesn't love me

ii) 'which', 'that' (referring to things):

j'ai perdu le briquet qu'il m'a offert
I've lost the lighter (which/that) he gave me

c) *qui* or *que*?

qui (subject) and **que** (object) are translated by the same words in English (who, which, that). To use the correct pronoun in French, it is essential to know whether a relative pronoun is the object or the subject of the relative clause:

i) when the verb of the relative clause has its own subject, the object pronoun **que** must be used:

c'est un passe-temps que j'adore
it's a pastime (that) I love *(the subject of 'adore' is 'je')*

ii) otherwise the relative pronoun is the subject of the verb in the relative clause and the subject pronoun **qui** must be used:

j'ai trouvé un manteau qui me plaît
I've found a coat that I like *(the subject of 'plaît' is 'qui')*

d) *LEQUEL*

i) forms

lequel (which) has four different forms, as it must agree with the noun to which it refers:

	SINGULAR	PLURAL	
MASCULINE	lequel	lesquels	} which
FEMININE	laquelle	lesquelles	

lequel etc combines with the prepositions **à** and **de** as follows:

à + lequel	→	auquel
à + lesquels	→	auxquels
à + lesquelles	→	auxquelles
de + lequel	→	duquel
de + lesquels	→	desquels
de + lesquelles	→	desquelles

à + laquelle and **de + laquelle** do not change.

> **quels sont les sports auxquels tu t'intéresses?**
> what sports are you interested *in*?

> **voilà le village près duquel on campait**
> here's the village which we camped near

ii) **qui** or **lequel** with a preposition?

When a relative pronoun follows a preposition, the pronoun used is either **qui** or **lequel**. In English, the relative pronoun is seldom used and the preposition is frequently placed after the verb or at the end of the sentence.

qui is generally used after a preposition when referring to people:

> **où est la fille *avec* qui je dansais?**
> where's the girl I was dancing *with*?

> **montre-moi la personnne *à* qui tu as vendu ton vélo**
> show me the person you sold your bike *to*

lequel is often used after a preposition when referring to things:

> **l'immeuble *dans* lequel j'habite est très moderne**
> the building (which) I live *in* is very modern

> **je ne reconnais pas la voiture *avec* laquelle il est venu**
> I don't recognize the car (which) he came *in*

lequel is also used when referring to persons after the prepositions **entre** (between) and **parmi** (among):

> **elle observait les invités parmi lesquels elle ne reconnaissait personne**
> she was watching the guests, none of whom she recognized

il y avait deux candidats, entre *lesquels* nous avons dû choisir
there were two candidates, between whom we had to choose

e) *DONT*

dont is frequently used instead of **de qui, duquel** etc. It means:

i) *of which/of whom:*

un métier dont il est fier
a job (which) he is proud of

Care must be taken with verbs that are normally followed by **de** + object: **de** is not always translated by 'of' in English, and is sometimes not translated at all (see section on verbal constructions pp 204-5):

voilà les choses *dont* j'ai besoin
here are the things (which) I need

les gens *dont* tu parles ne m'intéressent pas
I'm not interested in the people you're talking about

l'enfant *dont* elle s'occupe n'est pas le sien
the child she is looking *after* is not hers

ii) *whose*

dont is also used to translate the English pronoun 'whose'. In French, the construction of the clause that follows **dont** differs from English in two ways:

◻ the noun which follows **dont** is used with the definite article (**le, la, les, l'**):

mon copain, dont *le* père a eu un accident
my friend, whose father had an accident

◻ the word order in French is **dont** + subject + verb + object:

je te présente Hélène, dont tu connais déjà le frère
this is Hélène, whose brother you already know

c'était dans une petite rue dont j'ai oublié le nom
it was in a small street the name of which I've forgotten

Note that **dont** cannot be used after a preposition:

une jolie maison, *près* de laquelle il y a un petit lac
a pretty house, *next* to which there is a small lake

f) OÙ

i) **où** generally means 'where':

l'hôtel où on a logé était très confortable
the hotel where we stayed was very comfortable

ii) **où** often replaces a preposition + **lequel**, and means 'in/to/on/at which' etc:

c'est la maison où je suis né
that's the house in which/where I was born

une soirée où il a invité tous ses amis
a party to which he invited all his friends

iii) **où** is also used to translate 'when' after a noun referring to time:

le jour où	**la fois où**	**le moment où**
the day when	the time when	the moment when

tu te rappelles le soir où on a raté le dernier métro?
do you remember the evening when we missed the last train?

le jour où j'ai eu mon permis de conduire
the day when I got my driving licence

g) CE QUI, CE QUE

ce is used before **qui** and **que** when the relative pronoun does not refer to a specific noun. Both **ce qui** and **ce que** mean 'that which', 'the thing which', and are usually translated by 'what':

i) ce qui

ce qui is followed by a verb without a subject (**qui** is the subject):

ce qui s'est passé ne vous regarde pas
what happened is none of your business

ce qui m'étonne, c'est sa patience
what surprises me is his patience

Note that in French, this structure requires a comma between the two clauses, and the second clause must be introduced by **c'est/ c'était/ce sera** depending on the tense being used.

ii) ce que

ce que (**ce qu'** before a vowel or a silent **h**) is followed by a verb with its own subject (**que** is the object):

> **fais ce que tu veux**
> do what you want
>
> **c'est ce qu'il a dit?**
> is that what he said?
>
> **ce que vous me demandez est impossible**
> what you're asking me is impossible

iii) tout ce qui/que

tout is used in front of **ce qui/que** in the sense of 'all that', 'everything that':

> **c'est tout ce que je veux**
> that's all I want
>
> **tout ce que tu as fait**
> everything you did
>
> **tu n'as pas eu de mal; c'est tout ce qui compte**
> you weren't hurt; that's all that matters

iv) ce qui/que are often used in indirect questions (see p 76):

> **je ne sais pas ce qu'ils vont dire**
> I don't know what they'll say

v) when referring to a previous clause, **ce qui** and **ce que** are translated by 'which':

> **elle est en retard, ce qui arrive souvent**
> she's late, which happens often

vi) **ce qui/que** are used with a preposition; **ce qui** is used as the subject of the verb in the relative clause and **ce que** is used as the object of the verb in the relative clause:

> **ce n'est pas étonnant, après ce qui nous est arrivé**
> it's not surprising, after what happened to us
>
> **il y a du vrai dans ce que vous dites**
> there is some truth in what you say

When a preposition is required by the verb in the relative clause, eg **penser à**, **s'expliquer sur**, **quoi** is used instead of **ce que** and comes after the preposition:

> **c'est ce à quoi je pensais**
> that's what I was thinking about

voici ce sur quoi il devra s'expliquer
this is what he'll have to explain

ce dont is used instead of **de + ce que** when **de** is the preposition required by the verb in the relative clause, eg **avoir peur de, avoir besoin de**:

c'est ce dont j'avais peur
that's what I was afraid of

tu as trouvé ce dont tu avais besoin?
did you find what you needed?

7. VERBS

A. Regular Conjugations

1. Conjugations

There are three main conjugations in French, which are determined by the infinitive endings. The first conjugation verbs, by far the largest category, end in **-er**, eg aim**er** and will be referred to as **-er** verbs; the second conjugation verbs end in **-ir**, eg fin**ir** and will be referred to as **-ir** verbs; the third conjugation verbs, the smallest category, end in **-re**, eg vend**re** and will be referred to as **-re** verbs.

2. Simple tenses

The simple tenses in French are:

- ❑ present
- ❑ imperfect
- ❑ future
- ❑ conditional
- ❑ past historic
- ❑ present subjunctive
- ❑ imperfect subjunctive

For the use of the different tenses, see pp 126-33.

3. Formation of tenses

The tenses are formed by adding the following endings to the stem of the verb (usually the stem of the infinitive) as set out in the following section:

a)   *PRESENT*: stem of the infinitive + the following endings:

-er verbs	-ir verbs	-re verbs
-e, -es, -e,	-is, -is, -it,	-s, -s, ø,
-ons, -ez, -ent	-issons, -issez,	-ons, -ez, -ent
	-issent	

AIMER	FINIR	VENDRE
j'aime	je finis	je vends
tu aimes	tu finis	tu vends
il aime	il finit	il vend
elle aime	elle finit	elle vend
nous aimons	nous finissons	nous vendons
vous aimez	vous finissez	vous vendez
ils aiment	ils finissent	ils vendent
elles aiment	elles finissent	elles vendent

b) *IMPERFECT*: stem of the first person plural of the present indicative (ie the 'nous' form minus -ons) + the following endings:

-ais, -ais, -ait, -ions, -iez, -aient

j'aimais	je finissais	je vendais
tu aimais	tu finissais	tu vendais
il aimait	il finissait	il vendait
elle aimait	elle finissait	elle vendait
nous aimions	nous finissions	nous vendions
vous aimiez	vous finissiez	vous vendiez
ils aimaient	ils finissaient	ils vendaient
elles aimaient	elles finissaient	elles vendaient

Note that the only irregular imperfect is **être**: **j'étais** etc.

c) *FUTURE*: infinitive + the following endings:

-ai, -as, -a, -ons, -ez, -ont

Note that verbs ending in **-re** drop the final **e** of the infinitive.

j'aimerai	je finirai	je vendrai
tu aimeras	tu finiras	tu vendras
il aimera	il finira	il vendra
elle aimera	elle finira	elle vendra
nous aimerons	nous finirons	nous vendrons
vous aimerez	vous finirez	vous vendrez
ils aimeront	ils finiront	ils vendront
elles aimeront	elles finiront	elles vendront

d) *CONDITIONAL*: infinitive + the following endings:
-ais, -ais, -ait, -ions, -iez, -aient
Note that verbs ending in **-re** drop the final **e** of the infinitive.

j'aimer**ais**	je finir**ais**	je vendr**ais**
tu aimer**ais**	tu finir**ais**	tu vendr**ais**
il aimer**ait**	il finir**ait**	il vendr**ait**
elle aimer**ait**	elle finir**ait**	elle vendr**ait**
nous aimer**ions**	nous finir**ions**	nous vendr**ions**
vous aimer**iez**	vous finir**iez**	vous vendr**iez**
ils aimer**aient**	ils finir**aient**	ils vendr**aient**
elles aimer**aient**	elles finir**aient**	elles vendr**aient**

e) *PAST HISTORIC*: stem of the infinitive + the following endings:

-er verbs	**-ir** verbs	**-re** verbs
-ai, -as, -a,	**-is, -is, -it,**	**-is, -is, -it,**
-âmes, -âtes,	**-îmes, -îtes,**	**-îmes, -îtes,**
-èrent	**-irent**	**-irent**
j'aim**ai**	je fin**is**	je vend**is**
tu aim**as**	tu fin**is**	tu vend**is**
il aim**a**	il fin**it**	il vend**it**
elle aim**a**	elle fin**it**	elle vend**it**
nous aim**âmes**	nous fin**îmes**	nous vend**îmes**
vous aim**âtes**	vous fin**îtes**	vous vend**îtes**
ils aim**èrent**	ils fin**irent**	ils vend**irent**
elles aim**èrent**	elles fin**irent**	elles vend**irent**

f) *PRESENT SUBJUNCTIVE*: stem of the first person plural of the present indicative (ie the '**nous**' form minus **-ons**) + the following endings:

-e, -es, -e, -ions, -iez, -ent

j'aim**e**	je finiss**e**	je vend**e**
tu aim**es**	tu finiss**es**	tu vend**es**
il aim**e**	il finiss**e**	il vend**e**
elle aim**e**	elle finiss**e**	elle vend**e**
nous aim**ions**	nous finiss**ions**	nous vend**ions**
vous aim**iez**	vous finiss**iez**	vous vend**iez**
ils aim**ent**	ils finiss**ent**	ils vend**ent**
elles aim**ent**	elles finiss**ent**	elles vend**ent**

g) *IMPERFECT SUBJUNCTIVE*: stem of the first person singular of the past historic + the following endings:

-er verbs	**-ir** verbs	**-re** verbs
-asse, -asses, -ât, -assions, -assiez, -assent	**-isse, -isses, -ît, -issions, -issiez, -issent**	**-isse, -isses, -ît, -issions, -issiez, -issent**
j'aim**asse**	je fin**isse**	je vend**isse**
tu aim**asses**	tu fin**isses**	tu vend**isses**
il aim**ât**	il fin**ît**	il vend**ît**
elle aim**ât**	elle fin**ît**	elle vend**ît**
nous aim**assions**	nous fin**issions**	nous vend**issions**
vous aim**assiez**	vous fin**issiez**	vous vend**issiez**
ils aim**assent**	ils fin**issent**	ils vend**issent**
elles aim**assent**	elles fin**issent**	elles vend**issent**

B. Standard Spelling Irregularities

Spelling irregularities only affect **-er** verbs.

1. Verbs ending in -cer and -ger

a) Verbs ending in **-cer** require a cedilla under the **c** (**ç**) before an **a** or an **o** to preserve the soft sound of the **c**: eg **commencer** (to begin); **il commença** (he began).

b) Verbs ending in **-ger** require an **-e** after the **g** before an **a** or an **o** to preserve the soft sound of the **g**: eg **manger** (to eat); **je mangeais** (I was eating).

Changes to **-cer** and **-ger** verbs occur in the following tenses: present, imperfect, past historic, imperfect subjunctive and present participle.

COMMENCER	MANGER
PRESENT	
je commence	je mange
tu commences	tu manges
il commence	il mange
elle commence	elle mange
nous **commençons**	nous **mangeons**
vous commencez	vous mangez
ils commencent	ils mangent
elles commencent	elles mangent
IMPERFECT	
je **commençais**	je **mangeais**
tu **commençais**	tu **mangeais**
il **commençait**	il **mangeait**
elle **commençait**	elle **mangeait**
nous commencions	nous mangions
vous commenciez	vous mangiez
ils **commençaient**	ils **mangeaient**
elles **commençaient**	elles **mangeaient**

PAST HISTORIC

je **commençai**	je **mangeai**
tu **commenças**	tu **mangeas**
il **commença**	il **mangea**
elle **commença**	elle **mangea**
nous **commençâmes**	nous **mangeâmes**
vous **commençâtes**	vous **mangeâtes**
ils commencèrent	ils mangèrent
elles commencèrent	elles mangèrent

IMPERFECT SUBJUNCTIVE

je **commençasse**	je **mangeasse**
tu **commençasses**	tu **mangeasses**
il **commençât**	il **mangeât**
elle **commençât**	elle **mangeât**
nous **commençassions**	nous **mangeassions**
vous **commençassiez**	vous **mangeassiez**
ils **commençassent**	ils **mangeassent**
elles **commençassent**	elles **mangeassent**

PRESENT PARTICIPLE

commençant	**mangeant**

2. Verbs with other -er endings

a) Verbs ending in **-eler**

Verbs ending in **-eler** double the l before a silent **e** (ie before **-e, -es, -ent** of the present indicative and subjunctive, and throughout the future and present conditional): eg **appeler** (to call).

PRESENT INDICATIVE	PRESENT SUBJUNCTIVE
j'appelle	j'appelle
tu appelles	tu appelles
il appelle	il appelle
elle appelle	elle appelle
nous appelons	nous appelions
vous appelez	vous appeliez
ils appellent	ils appellent
elles appellent	elles appellent

FUTURE	CONDITIONAL
j'appellerai	j'appellerais
tu appelleras	tu appellerais
il appellera	il appellerait
elle appellera	elle appellerait
nous appellerons	nous appellerions
vous appellerez	vous appelleriez
ils appelleront	ils appelleraient
elles appelleront	elles appelleraient

Note, however, that some verbs in **-eler**, including the following, are conjugated like **acheter** (see p 109):

celer	to conceal
congeler	to (deep-)freeze
déceler	to detect, to reveal
dégeler	to defrost
geler	to freeze
harceler	to harass
marteler	to hammer
modeler	to model
peler	to peel

b) Verbs ending in **-eter**

Verbs ending in **-eter** double the **t** before a silent **e** (ie before **-e, -es, -ent** of the present indicative and subjunctive, and throughout the future and conditional): eg **jeter** (to throw).

PRESENT INDICATIVE	*PRESENT SUBJUNCTIVE*
je **jette**	je **jette**
tu **jettes**	tu **jettes**
il **jette**	il **jette**
elle **jette**	elle **jette**
nous jetons	nous jetions
vous jetez	vous jetiez
ils **jettent**	ils **jettent**
elles **jettent**	elles **jettent**

FUTURE	*CONDITIONAL*
je **jetterai**	je **jetterais**
tu **jetteras**	tu **jetterais**
il **jettera**	il **jetterait**
elle **jettera**	elle **jetterait**
nous **jetterons**	nous **jetterions**
vous **jetterez**	vous **jetteriez**
ils **jetteront**	ils **jetteraient**
elles **jetteront**	elles **jetteraient**

Note, however, that some verbs in **-eter**, including the following, are conjugated like **acheter** (see p 109):

crocheter	to pick *(a lock)*
fureter	to ferret about
haleter	to pant
racheter	to buy back

VERBS

c) Verbs ending in **-oyer** and **-uyer**

In verbs ending in **-oyer** and **-uyer** the **y** changes to **i** before a silent **e** (ie before **-e**, **-es**, **-ent** of the present indicative and subjunctive, and throughout the future and conditional): eg **employer** (to use) and **ennuyer** (to bore).

PRESENT INDICATIVE	*PRESENT SUBJUNCTIVE*
j'**emploie**	j'**emploie**
tu **emploies**	tu **emploies**
il **emploie**	il **emploie**
elle **emploie**	elle **emploie**
nous **employons**	nous **employions**
vous **employez**	vous **employiez**
ils **emploient**	ils **emploient**
elles **emploient**	elles **emploient**

FUTURE	*CONDITIONAL*
j'**emploierai**	j'**emploierais**
tu **emploieras**	tu **emploierais**
il **emploiera**	il **emploierait**
elle **emploiera**	elle **emploierait**
nous **emploierons**	nous **emploierions**
vous **emploierez**	vous **emploieriez**
ils **emploieront**	ils **emploieraient**
elles **emploieront**	elles **emploieraient**

Note that **envoyer** (to send) and **renvoyer** (to dismiss) have an irregular future and conditional: j'**enverrai**, j'**enverrais**; je **renverrai**, je **renverrais**.

d) Verbs ending in **-ayer**

In verbs ending in **-ayer**, eg **balayer** (to sweep), **payer** (to pay), **essayer** (to try), the change from **y** to **i** is optional:

eg	je **balaie**	*or*	je **balaye**
	je **paie**	*or*	je **paye**
	j'**essaie**	*or*	j'**essaye**

e) Verbs in e- + consonant + -er

Verbs like **acheter, enlever, mener, peser** change the (last) **e** of the stem to **è** before a silent **e** (ie before **-e, -es, -ent** of the present indicative and subjunctive and throughout the future and conditional):

PRESENT INDICATIVE

j'**achète**
tu **achètes**
il **achète**
elle **achète**
nous achetons
vous achetez
ils **achètent**
elles **achètent**

PRESENT SUBJUNCTIVE

j'**achète**
tu **achètes**
il **achète**
elle **achète**
nous achetions
vous achetiez
ils **achètent**
elles **achètent**

FUTURE

j'**achèterai**
tu **achèteras**
il **achètera**
elle **achètera**
nous **achèterons**
vous **achèterez**
ils **achèteront**
elles **achèteront**

CONDITIONAL

j'**achèterais**
tu **achèterais**
il **achèterait**
elle **achèterait**
nous **achèterions**
vous **achèteriez**
ils **achèteraient**
elles **achèteraient**

Verbs conjugated like **acheter** include:

achever to complete
amener to bring
celer to conceal
crever to burst
crocheter to pick *(lock)*
élever to raise
emmener to take away
enlever to remove
étiqueter to label
fureter to ferret about
geler to freeze

haleter to pant
harceler to harass
lever to lift
marteler to hammer
mener to lead
modeler to model
peler to peel
peser to weigh
se promener to go for a walk
semer to sow
soulever to lift

VERBS

f) Verbs in **é-** + consonant + **-er**

Verbs like **espérer** (to hope) change **é** to **è** before a silent **e** in the present indicative and subjunctive. Note, however, that in the future and conditional **é** is retained.

PRESENT INDICATIVE

j'**espère**
tu **espères**
il **espère**
elle **espère**
nous espérons
vous espérez
ils **espèrent**
elles **espèrent**

PRESENT SUBJUNCTIVE

j'**espère**
tu **espères**
il **espère**
elle **espère**
nous espérions
vous espériez
ils **espèrent**
elles **espèrent**

FUTURE

j'**espérerai**
tu **espéreras**
il **espérera**
elle **espérera**
nous **espérerons**
vous **espérerez**
ils **espéreront**
elles **espéreront**

CONDITIONAL

j'**espérerais**
tu **espérerais**
il **espérerait**
elle **espérerait**
nous **espérerions**
vous **espéreriez**
ils **espéreraient**
elles **espéreraient**

Verbs conjugated like **espérer** include verbs in **-éder, -érer, -éter** etc:

accéder	to accede to
céder	to yield
célébrer	to celebrate
compléter	to complete
considérer	to consider
décéder	to die
digérer	to digest
gérer	to manage
inquiéter	to worry
libérer	to free
opérer	to operate
pénétrer	to penetrate

persévérer	to persevere
posséder	to possess
précéder	to precede
préférer	to prefer
protéger	to protect
récupérer	to recover
refréner	to curb
régler	to rule
régner	to reign
répéter	to repeat, to rehearse
révéler	to reveal
sécher	to dry
succéder	to succeed
suggérer	to suggest
tolérer	to tolerate

C. Auxiliaries And The Formation Of Compound Tenses

1. Formation

a) The two auxiliary verbs **avoir** and **être** are used with the past participle of a verb to form compound tenses.

b) *The past participle*

The regular past participle is formed by taking the stem of the infinitive and adding the following endings:

-er	-ir	-re
aim(er) + é	fin(ir) + i	vend(re) + u
aimé	fini	vendu

For the agreement of past participles see pp 158-60.

c) *Compound tenses*

In French there are seven compound tenses: perfect, pluperfect, future perfect, past conditional (conditional perfect), past anterior, perfect subjunctive, pluperfect subjunctive.

2. Verbs conjugated with AVOIR

PERFECT

present of **avoir** +
past participle

j'ai aimé
tu as aimé
il a aimé
elle a aimé
nous avons aimé
vous avez aimé
ils ont aimé
elles ont aimé

PLUPERFECT

imperfect of **avoir** +
past participle

j'avais aimé
tu avais aimé
il avait aimé
elle avait aimé
nous avions aimé
vous aviez aimé
ils avaient aimé
elles avaient aimé

FUTURE PERFECT

future of **avoir** +
past participle

j'aurai aimé
tu auras aimé
il aura aimé
elle aura aimé
nous aurons aimé
vous aurez aimé
ils auront aimé
elles auront aimé

PAST ANTERIOR

past historic of **avoir** +
past participle

j'eus aimé
tu eus aimé
il eut aimé
elle eut aimé
nous eûmes aimé
vous eûtes aimé
ils eurent aimé
elles eurent aimé

PERFECT SUBJUNCTIVE

present subjunctive of
avoir + past participle

j'aie aimé
tu aies aimé
il ait aimé
elle ait aimé
nous ayons aimé
vous ayez aimé
ils aient aimé
elles aient aimé

PAST CONDITIONAL

conditional of **avoir** +
past participle

j'aurais aimé
tu aurais aimé
il aurait aimé
elle aurait aimé
nous aurions aimé
vous auriez aimé
ils auraient aimé
elles auraient aimé

PLUPERFECT SUBJUNCTIVE

imperfect subjunctive of
avoir + past participle

j'eusse aimé
tu eusses aimé
il eût aimé
elle eût aimé
nous eussions aimé
vous eussiez aimé
ils eussent aimé
elles eussent aimé

3. Verbs conjugated with ÊTRE

PERFECT

present of **être** +
past participle

je suis arrivé(e)
tu es arrivé(e)
il est arrivé
elle est arrivée
nous sommes arrivé(e)s
vous êtes arrivé(e)(s)
ils sont arrivés
elles sont arrivées

FUTURE PERFECT

future of **être** +
past participle

je serai arrivé(e)
tu seras arrivé(e)
il sera arrivé
elle sera arrivée
nous serons arrivé(e)s
vous serez arrivé(e)(s)
ils seront arrivés
elles seront arrivées

PAST ANTERIOR

past historic of **être** +
past participle

je fus arrivé(e)
tu fus arrivé(e)
il fut arrivé
elle fut arrivée
nous fûmes arrivé(e)s
vous fûtes arrivé(e)(s)
ils furent arrivés
elles furent arrivées

PLUPERFECT

imperfect of **être** +
past participle

j'étais arrivé(e)
tu étais arrivé(e)
il était arrivé
elle était arrivée
nous étions arrivé(e)s
vous étiez arrivé(e)(s)
ils étaient arrivés
elles étaient arrivées

PAST CONDITIONAL

conditional of **être** +
past participle

je serais arrivé(e)
tu serais arrivé(e)
il serait arrivé
elle serait arrivée
nous serions arrivé(e)s
vous seriez arrivé(e)(s)
ils seraient arrivés
elles seraient arrivées

PERFECT SUBJUNCTIVE	PLUPERFECT SUBJUNCTIVE
present subjunctive of **être** + past participle	imperfect subjunctive of **être** + past participle

je sois arrivé(e)	je fusse arrivé(e)
tu sois arrivé(e)	tu fusses arrivé(e)
il soit arrivé	il fût arrivé
elle soit arrivée	elle fût arrivée
nous soyons arrivé(e)s	nous fussions arrivé(e)s
vous soyez arrivé(e)(s)	vous fussiez arrivé(e)(s)
ils soient arrivés	ils fussent arrivés
elles soient arrivées	elles fussent arrivées

4. AVOIR or ÊTRE?

a) *Verbs conjugated with **avoir***

The compound tenses of most verbs are formed with **avoir**:

j'ai marqué un but	elle a dansé toute la nuit
I scored a goal	she danced all night

b) *Verbs conjugated with **être***

i) all reflexive verbs (see p 119):

je me suis baigné
I had a bath

ii) the following verbs (mainly of motion):

aller	to go
arriver	to arrive
descendre	to go/come down
entrer	to go/come in
monter	to go/come up
mourir	to die
naître	to be born
partir	to leave
passer	to go through, to drop in
rester	to remain

115

retourner	to return
sortir	to go/come out
tomber	to fall
venir	to come

and most of their compounds:

revenir	to come back
devenir	to become
parvenir	to reach, to manage to
rentrer	to return home
remonter	to go up again
redescendre	to go down again

Note, however, that **prévenir** (to warn) and **subvenir** (to provide for) are conjugated with **avoir**:

> **je t'avais prévenu!**
> I did warn you!

> **elle avait subvenu à toutes les dépenses**
> she met all the expenses

Note too that **passer** can also be conjugated with **avoir**:

> **il a passé par Paris**
> he went via Paris

Some of the verbs listed above can take a direct object. In such cases they are conjugated with **avoir** and will have a different meaning:

descendre	to take/bring down, to go down *(the stairs, a slope)*
monter	to take/bring up, to go up *(the stairs, a slope)*
rentrer	to take/bring/put in
retourner	to turn over
sortir	to take/bring out

> **les élèves sont sortis à midi**
> the pupils came out at midday

> **les élèves ont sorti leurs livres**
> the pupils took out their books

116

VERBS

elle n'est pas encore descendue
she hasn't come down yet

elle a descendu un vieux tableau du grenier
she brought an old painting down from the loft

elle a descendu l'escalier
she came down the stairs

les prisonniers sont montés sur le toit
the prisoners climbed on to the roof

le garçon a monté les bouteilles de vin de la cave
the waiter brought the bottles of wine up from the cellar

nous sommes rentrés tard
we got home late

j'ai rentré la voiture dans le garage
I put the car in the garage

je serais retourné à Paris
I would have returned to Paris

le jardinier a retourné le sol
the gardener turned over the soil

ils sont sortis de la piscine
they got out of the swimming pool

il a sorti les mains de ses poches
he took his hands out of his pockets

D. Reflexive Verbs

1. Definition

Reflexive verbs are so called because they 'reflect' the action back onto the subject. Reflexive verbs are always accompanied by a reflexive pronoun, eg in the following sentence:

I look at myself in the mirror

'myself' is the reflexive pronoun.

je lave la voiture I'm washing the car	**je me lave** I'm washing *myself*
j'ai couché le bébé I put the baby to bed	**je me suis couché** I went to bed (I put *myself* to bed)

2. Reflexive pronouns

They are:

PERSON	SINGULAR	PLURAL
1st	**me (m')** myself	**nous** ourselves
2nd	**te (t')** yourself	**vous** yourself/selves
3rd	**se (s')** himself, herself, itself, oneself	**se (s')** themselves

Note:

a) **m'**, **t'** and **s'** are used instead of **me, te** and **se** in front of a vowel or a silent **h**:

   tu t'amuses? – non, je m'ennuie
   are you enjoying yourself? – no, I'm bored

   il s'habille dans la salle de bain
   he gets dressed in the bathroom

b) French reflexive pronouns are often not translated in English:

   je me demande si …   **ils se moquent de moi**
   I wonder if …   they're making fun of me

c) Plural reflexive pronouns can also be used to express reciprocal actions; in this case they are translated by 'each other' or 'one another':

nous nous détestons	**ils ne se parlent pas**
we hate one another	they're not talking to each other

d) **se** can mean 'ourselves' or 'each other' when it is used with the pronoun **on** meaning 'we' (see p 71):

on s'est perdu	**on se connaît**
we got lost	we know each other

3. Position of reflexive pronouns

Reflexive pronouns are placed immediately before the verb, except in positive commands, where they follow the verb and are linked to it by a hyphen:

tu te dépêches?	**dépêchons-nous!**
will you hurry up?	let's hurry!
ne t'inquiète pas	**ne vous fiez pas à lui**
don't worry	don't trust him

Note that reflexive pronouns change to emphatic (disjunctive) pronouns in positive commands:

elle doit se reposer	**repose-toi**
she needs to rest	have a rest

4. Conjugation of reflexive verbs

a) *Simple tenses*

These are conjugated in the same way as non-reflexive verbs, except that a reflexive pronoun is used.

b) *Compound tenses*

These are conjugated using the auxiliary **être** followed by the past participle of the verb.

A full conjugation table is given on p 187.

5. Agreement of the past participle

a) In most cases, the reflexive pronoun is a direct object and the past
participle of the verb agrees in number and in gender with
the reflexive pronoun:

il s'est trompé
he made a mistake

elle s'est endormie
she fell asleep

ils se sont excusés
they apologized

elles se sont assises
they sat down

b) When the reflexive pronoun is used as an indirect object, the past
participle does not change:

nous nous sommes écrit
we wrote to each other

elle se l'est acheté
she bought it for herself

elles se sont parlé
they spoke to each other

les années se sont succédé
one year followed another

When the reflexive verb has a direct object, the reflexive pronoun is
the indirect object of the reflexive verb and the past participle does
not agree with it:

Caroline s'est tordu la cheville
Caroline sprained her ankle

vous vous êtes lavé les mains, les filles?
did you wash your hands, girls?

elles se sont égratigné les genoux
they scratched their knees

6. Common reflexive verbs

s'en aller to go away	**s'éloigner (de)** to move away (from)	**se moquer de** to laugh at
s'amuser to have fun	**s'endormir** to fall asleep	**s'occuper de** to take care of
s'appeler to be called	**s'ennuyer** to be bored	**se passer** to happen

s'approcher (de)
to come near

s'arrêter
to stop

s'asseoir
to sit down

s'attendre à
to expect

se baigner
to have a bath

se battre
to fight

se blesser
to hurt oneself

se coucher
to go to bed

se débarrasser de
to get rid of

se demander
to wonder

se dépêcher
to hurry

se déshabiller
to undress

se diriger vers
to move towards

s'étonner (de)
to be surprised (at)

s'excuser (de)
to apologize (for)

se fâcher
to get angry/fall out

s'écrier
to cry out/exclaim

s'habiller
to get dressed

se hâter
to hurry

s'inquiéter
to worry

s'installer
to settle down

se laver
to wash

se lever
to get up

se mêler de
to meddle with

se mettre à
to start

se mettre en route
to set off

se passer de
to do without

se promener
to go for a walk

se rappeler
to remember

se raser
to shave

se renseigner
to make enquiries

se ressembler
to look alike

se retourner
to turn round

se réveiller
to wake up

se sauver
to run away

se souvenir (de)
to remember

se taire
to be/keep quiet

se tromper
to be mistaken

se trouver
to be (situated)

E. Impersonal Verbs

1. Conjugation

Impersonal verbs are used only in the third person singular and in the infinitive. The subject is always the impersonal pronoun **il** (= it).

il neige	**il y a du brouillard**
it's snowing	it's foggy

2. List of impersonal verbs

a) *verbs describing the weather:*

i) **faire** + adjective:

il fait beau/chaud	**il fait frais/froid**
it's fine/warm	it's cool/cold
il fera beau demain	**il va faire très froid**
the weather will be good tomorrow	it will be very cold

ii) **faire** + noun:

il fait beau temps	**il fait mauvais temps**
the weather is nice	the weather is bad
il fait jour	**il fait nuit**
it's daylight	it's dark

iii) other impersonal verbs and verbs used impersonally to describe the weather:

il gèle	**(geler)**	it's freezing
il grêle	**(grêler)**	it's hailing
il neige	**(neiger)**	it's snowing
il pleut	**(pleuvoir)**	it's raining
il tonne	**(tonner)**	there's thunder

Note that some of these verbs may be used personally:

je gèle	I'm freezing

iv) **il y a** + noun:

il y a des nuages	it's cloudy
il y a du brouillard	it's foggy
il y a du verglas	it's icy

b) *être*

i) **il est** + noun:

il est cinq heures
it's five o'clock

il était une fois un géant
once upon a time there was a
giant

ii) **il est** + adjective + **de** + infinitive:

il est difficile de	it's difficult to
il est facile de	it's easy to
il est nécessaire de	it's necessary to
il est inutile de	it's useless to
il est possible de	it's possible to

il est difficile d'en parler
it's difficult to talk about it

Note that the indirect object pronoun in French corresponds to the
English 'for me', 'for him' etc:

il m'est difficile d'en parler
it's difficult for me to talk about it

iii) **il est** + adjective + **que**:

il est douteux que	it's doubtful that
il est évident que	it's clear that
il est possible que	it's possible that
il est probable que	it's probable that
il est peu probable que	it's unlikely that
il est vrai que	it's true that

Note that **que** may be followed by the indicative or the subjunctive
(see p 126):

il est probable qu'il ne viendra pas
he probably won't come

il est peu probable qu'il vienne
it's unlikely that he'll come

c) *arriver, se passer (to happen)*

il est arrivé une chose curieuse
a strange thing happened

que se passe-t-il?
what's happening?

d) *exister (to exist), rester (to remain), manquer (to be missing)*

il existe trois exemplaires de ce livre
there are three copies of this book

il me restait un euro
I had one euro left

il me manque 4 euros
I am 4 euros short

e) *paraître, sembler (to seem)*

il paraîtrait/semblerait qu'il ait changé d'avis
it would appear that he has changed his mind

il paraît qu'il va se marier
it seems he's going to get married

il me semble que le professeur s'est trompé
it seems to me that the teacher has made a mistake

f) *other common impersonal verbs*

i) **s'agir** (to be a matter of) may be followed by a noun, a pronoun or an infinitive:

il s'agit de ton avenir
it's about your future

de quoi s'agit-il?
what's it about?

il s'agit de trouver le coupable
we must find the culprit

ii) **falloir** (to be necessary) may be followed by a noun, an infinitive or the subjunctive:

il faut deux heures pour aller à Paris
it takes two hours to get to Paris

il me faut plus de temps
I need more time

il faudra rentrer plus tôt ce soir
we'll have to come home earlier tonight

il faut que tu parles à Papa
you have to speak to Dad

iii) **suffire** (to be enough) may be followed by a noun, an infinitive or the subjunctive:

il suffit de peu de chose pour être heureux
it doesn't take much to be happy

il suffit de passer le pont
you only have to cross the bridge

il suffira qu'ils te donnent le numéro de téléphone
they will only have to give you the telephone number

iv) **valoir mieux** (to be better) may be followed by an infinitive or the subjunctive:

il vaudrait mieux prendre le car
it would be better to take the coach

il vaut mieux que vous ne sortiez pas seule le soir
you'd better not go out alone at night

F. Tenses

For the formation of the different tenses, see pp 100-3 and 112-5.

Note that French has no continuous tenses (as in 'I am eating', 'I was going', 'I will be arriving'). The 'be' and '-ing' parts of English continuous tenses are not translated as separate words. Instead, the equivalent tense is used in French:

je mange
I am eating

je mangerai
I will be eating

1. PRESENT

The present is used to describe what someone does/something that happens regularly, or what someone is doing/something that is happening at the time of speaking.

a) *regular actions*

il travaille dans un bureau
he works in an office

je lis rarement le journal
I seldom read the paper

b) *continuous actions*

ne le dérangez pas, il travaille
don't disturb him, he's working

je ne peux pas venir, je garde mon petit frère
I can't come, I'm looking after my little brother

Note that the continuous nature of the action can also be expressed by using the phrase **être en train de** (to be in the process of) + infinitive:

je suis en train de cuisiner
I'm (busy) cooking

c) *immediate future*

je pars demain
I'm leaving tomorrow

However, the present cannot be used after **quand** and other conjunctions of time when the future is implied (see p 129):

> **je le ferai quand j'aurai le temps**
> I'll do it when I have the time

d) *general truths*

> **la vie est dure**
> life is hard

2. IMPERFECT

The imperfect is a past tense used to express what someone was doing or what someone used to do, or to describe something in the past. The imperfect refers particularly to something that *continued* over a period of time, as opposed to something that happened at a specific point in time.

a) *continuous actions*

the imperfect describes an action that was happening, often when something else took place:

> **il prenait un bain quand le téléphone a sonné**
> he was having a bath when the phone rang

> **excuse-moi, je pensais à autre chose**
> I'm sorry, I was thinking of something else

Note that the continuous nature of the action can be emphasized by using **être en train de** + infinitive:

> **j'étais en train de faire le ménage**
> I was (busy) doing the housework

b) *regular actions in the past*

> **je le voyais souvent quand il habitait dans le quartier**
> I used to see him often when he lived in this area

> **quand il était plus jeune il voyageait beaucoup**
> when he was younger he used to travel a lot

c) *description in the past*

> **il faisait beau ce jour-là**   **c'était formidable!**
> the weather was good that day   it was great!

> **elle portait une robe bleue**   **elle donnait sur la rue**
> she wore a blue dress   it looked onto the street

3. PERFECT

The perfect tense is a compound past tense, used to express *single* actions which have been completed. What someone did, has done or has been doing, or something that has happened or has been happening are all expressed using the perfect tense:

je l'ai envoyé lundi
I sent it on Monday

on est sorti hier soir
we went out last night

tu t'es bien amusé?
did you have a good time?

je ne l'ai pas vu de toute la journée
I haven't seen him all day

j'ai lu toute la journée
I've been reading all day

tu as déjà mangé?
have you eaten?

In English, the simple past ('did', 'went', 'prepared') is used to describe both single and repeated actions in the past. In French, the perfect only describes single actions in the past, while repeated actions are expressed by the imperfect (they are sometimes signposted by 'used to'). Thus 'I went' should be translated 'j'allais' or 'je suis allé' depending on the nature of the action:

après dîner, je suis allé en ville
after dinner I went into town

l'an dernier, j'allais plus souvent au théâtre
last year I went to the theatre more often

4. PAST HISTORIC

This tense is used in the same way as the perfect tense, to describe a single, completed action in the past (what someone did or something that happened). It is a literary tense, not common in everyday spoken French; it is found mainly as a narrative tense in written form:

le piéton ne vit pas arriver la voiture
the pedestrian didn't see the car coming

5. PLUPERFECT

This compound tense is used to express what someone had done/had been doing or something that had happened or had been happening:

il n'avait pas voulu aller avec eux
he hadn't wanted to go with them

elle était essoufflée parce qu'elle avait couru
she was out of breath because she'd been running

However, the pluperfect is not used as in English with **depuis** (for, since), or with **venir de** + infinitive (to have just done something). For details see pp 130-3:

il neigeait depuis une semaine
it had been snowing for a week

les pompiers venaient d'arriver
the firemen had just arrived

6. FUTURE

This tense is used to express what someone will do or will be doing or something that will happen or will be happening:

je ferai la vaisselle demain   **j'arriverai tard**
I'll do the dishes tomorrow   I'll be arriving late

Note that the future and not the present, as in English, is used in time clauses introduced by **quand** (when) or other conjunctions of time where the future is implied (see p 129):

il viendra quand il le pourra
he'll come when he can

French makes frequent use of **aller** + infinitive (to be about to do something) to express the immediate future:

je vais vous expliquer ce qui s'est passé
I'll explain (to you) what happened

il va déménager la semaine prochaine
he's moving house next week

7. FUTURE PERFECT

This compound tense is used to describe what someone will have done or will have been doing in the future or to describe something that will have happened in the future:

j'aurai bientôt fini
I will soon have finished

In particular, it is used instead of the English perfect in time clauses introduced by **quand** or other conjunctions of time where the future is implied (see p 129):

appelle-moi quand tu auras fini
call me when you've finished

on rentrera dès qu'on aura fait les courses
we'll come back as soon as we've done the shopping

8. PAST ANTERIOR

This tense is used instead of the pluperfect to express an action that preceded another action in the past (ie a past in the past). It is usually introduced by a conjunction of time (translated by 'when', 'as soon as', 'after' etc) and the main verb is in the past historic:

il se coucha dès qu'ils furent partis
he went to bed as soon as they'd left

à peine eut-elle raccroché que le téléphone sonna
she'd hardly hung up when the telephone rang

9. Use of tenses with 'depuis' (for, since)

a) The present must be used instead of the perfect to describe actions which started in the past and are still continuing:

il habite ici depuis trois ans
he's been living here for three years

elle t'attend depuis ce matin
she's been waiting for you since this morning

Note, however, that the perfect, not the present, is used when the clause is negative or when the action has been completed:

il n'a pas pris de vacances depuis longtemps
he hasn't taken any holidays for a long time

j'ai fini depuis un bon moment
I've been finished for quite a while

Note:

i) **il y a … que** or **voilà … que** are also used with the present tense to translate 'for':

it's been ringing for ten minutes
ça sonne depuis dix minutes
il y a dix minutes que ça sonne
voilà dix minutes que ça sonne

ii) **depuis que** is used when 'since' introduces a clause, ie when there is a verb following **depuis**:

elle dort depuis que vous êtes partis
she's been sleeping since you left

iii) Do not confuse **depuis** (for, since) and **pendant** (for, during): **depuis** refers to the starting point of an action which is still going on and **pendant** refers to the duration of an action which is over and is used with the perfect:

il vit ici depuis deux mois
he's been living here for two months

il a vécu ici pendant deux mois
he lived here for two months

b) The imperfect must be used instead of the pluperfect to describe an action which had started in the past and was still going on at a given time:

elle le connaissait depuis son enfance
she had known him since her childhood

il attendait depuis trois heures quand on est arrivé
he had been waiting for three hours when we arrived

Note, however, that if the sentence is negative or if the action has been completed, the pluperfect and not the imperfect is used:

je n'étais pas allé au théâtre depuis des années
I hadn't been to the theatre for years

il était parti depuis peu
he'd been gone for a short while

Note:

i) **il y avait ... que** + imperfect is also used to translate 'for':

she'd been living alone for a long time
elle habitait seule depuis longtemps
il y avait longtemps qu'elle habitait seule

ii) **depuis que** is used when 'since' introduces a clause; if it describes an action which was still going on at the time, it can be followed by the imperfect, otherwise it is followed by the pluperfect:

il pleuvait depuis que nous étions en vacances
it had been raining since we had been on holiday

il pleuvait depuis que nous étions arrivés
it had been raining since we arrived

iii) Do not confuse **depuis** and **pendant**: **depuis** refers to the starting point of an action which is still going on and **pendant** refers to the duration of an action which is over; **pendant** is used with the pluperfect:

j'y travaillais depuis un an
I had been working there for a year

j'y avais travaillé pendant un an
I had worked there for a year

10. Use of tenses with 'venir de'

venir de + infinitive means 'to have just done'.

a) If it describes something that has just happened, it is used in the present instead of the perfect:

l'avion vient d'arriver
the plane has just arrived

je viens de te le dire!
I've just told you!

b) If it describes something that had just happened, it is used in the imperfect instead of the pluperfect:

le film venait de commencer   je venais de rentrer
the film had just started   I'd just got home

11. Use of tenses after conjunctions of time

quand	when
tant que	as long as
dès/aussitôt que	as soon as
lorsque	when
pendant que	while

Verbs which follow these conjunctions must be used in the following tenses:

a) *future instead of present:*

je te téléphonerai quand je serai prêt
I'll phone you when I'm ready

elle ira le voir dès qu'elle le pourra
she'll go to see him as soon as she can

b) *future perfect instead of perfect* when the future is implied:

on rentrera dès qu'on aura fini les courses
we'll come back as soon as we've done the shopping

je t'appellerai dès qu'il sera arrivé
I'll call you as soon as he's arrived

c) *conditional present/perfect instead of perfect/pluperfect* in indirect speech:

il a dit qu'il sortirait quand il aurait fini
he said that he would come out when he had finished

For the tenses of the subjunctive and conditional, see pp 134-8 and 141-2.

G. Moods

1. THE SUBJUNCTIVE

In everyday spoken French, the only two subjunctive tenses that are used are the present and the perfect. The imperfect and the pluperfect subjunctive are found mainly in literature or in texts of a formal nature.

The subjunctive is always preceded by the conjunction **que** and is used in subordinate clauses when the subject of the subordinate clause is different from the subject of the main verb.

Some clauses introduced by **que** take the indicative. The subjunctive must be used after the following:

a) Verbs of emotion

être content que	to be pleased that
être désolé que	to be sorry that
être étonné que	to be surprised that
être heureux que	to be happy that
être surpris que	to be surprised that
être triste que	to be sad that
avoir peur que … ne	to be afraid/to fear that
craindre que … ne	to be afraid/to fear that
regretter que	to be sorry that

ils étaient contents que j'aille les voir
they were pleased (that) I went to visit them

je serais très étonné qu'il mente
I would be very surprised if he was lying

je regrette que tu ne puisses pas y aller
I'm sorry (that) you can't go

Note that **ne** is used after several verbs in the subjunctive mood but it does not have a negative meaning in itself and is not translated in English:

je crains que l'avion *ne* soit en retard
I'm afraid (that) the plane will be late

j'ai bien peur qu'il *ne* soit déjà trop tard
I'm very much afraid (that) it's already too late

pour éviter que la situation *ne* s'aggrave
to prevent the situation from getting any worse

b) Verbs of wishing and willing:

aimer que	to like
désirer que	to wish (that)
préférer que	to prefer (that)
souhaiter que	to wish (that)
vouloir que	to want

Note that in English, such verbs are often used in the following type of construction: verb of willing + object + infinitive (eg I'd like you to listen); this type of construction is impossible in French, where a subjunctive clause has to be used:

je souhaite que tu réussisses
I hope you will succeed

il aimerait que je lui écrive plus souvent
he'd like me to write to him more often

voulez-vous que je vous y amène en voiture?
would you like me to drive you there?

préférez-vous que je rappelle demain?
would you rather I called back tomorrow?

c) Impersonal constructions (expressing necessity, possibility, doubt, denial, preference):

il faut que	it is necessary (that) *(must)*
il est nécessaire que	it is necessary that *(must)*
il est important que	it is important (that)
il est possible que	it is possible that *(may)*
il se peut que	it is possible that *(may)*
il est impossible que	it is impossible (that) *(can't)*
il est douteux que	it is doubtful whether
il est peu probable que	it is unlikely that
il semble que	it seems (that)
il est préférable que	it is preferable (that)
il vaut mieux que	it is better (that) *(had better)*
c'est dommage que	it is a pity (that)

VERBS

Note that these expressions may be used in any appropriate tense:

il faut absolument que je le leur dise
I simply must tell them

il était important que tu le saches
it was important that you should know

il se pourrait qu'elle change d'avis
she might change her mind

il est peu probable qu'ils s'y intéressent
they're unlikely to be interested in that

il semble qu'elle ait raison
she appears to be right

il vaudrait mieux que tu ne promettes rien
you'd better not promise anything

c'est dommage que vous vous soyez manqués
it's a pity you missed each other

d) Some verbs and impersonal constructions expressing doubt or uncertainty (mainly used negatively or interrogatively):

douter que	to doubt (that)
(ne pas) croire que	(not) to believe (that)
(ne pas) penser que	(not) to think (that)
(ne pas) être sûr que	(not) to be sure that
il n'est pas certain que	it isn't certain that
il n'est pas évident que	it isn't obvious that
il n'est pas sûr que	it isn't certain that
il n'est pas vrai que	it isn't true that

je doute fort qu'il veuille t'aider
I very much doubt whether he'll want to help you

croyez-vous qu'il y ait des places libres?
do you think there are any seats available?

on n'était pas sûr que ce soit le bon endroit
we weren't sure that it was the right place

il n'était pas certain qu'elle puisse gagner
it wasn't certain whether she could win

e) **attendre que** (to wait until someone does something or something
  happens, to wait for someone to do something or for something to
  happen):

> **attendons qu'il revienne**
> let's wait until he comes back

f) Some subordinating conjunctions:

bien que	although
quoique	although
sans que	without
pour que	so that
afin que	so that
à condition que	provided that
pourvu que	provided that
jusqu'à ce que	until
en attendant que	until
avant que … (ne)	before
à moins que … (ne)	unless
de peur que … ne	for fear that
de crainte que … ne	for fear that
de sorte que	so that
de façon que	so that
de manière que	so that

Note that when **ne** is shown in brackets, it may follow the
conjunction, although it is seldom used in spoken French; it does not
have a negative meaning, and is not translated in English.

> **il est allé travailler bien qu'il soit malade**
> he went to work although he was ill

> **elle est entrée sans que je la voie**
> she came in without me seeing her

> **voilà de l'argent pour que tu puisses aller au cinéma**
> here's some money so that you can go to the cinema

> **d'accord, pourvu que tu me promettes de ne pas le répéter**
> all right, as long as you promise not to tell anyone

> **tu l'as revu avant qu'il (ne) parte?**
> did you see him again before he left?

je le ferai demain, à moins que ce (ne) soit urgent
I'll do it tomorrow, unless it's urgent

elle n'a pas fait de bruit de peur qu'il ne se réveille
she didn't make any noise in case he woke

parle moins fort de sorte qu'elle ne nous entende pas
talk more quietly so that she doesn't hear us

Note that when **de façon/manière que** (so that) expresses a result, as opposed to a purpose, the indicative is used instead of the subjunctive:

il a fait du bruit de sorte qu'elle l'*a entendu*
he made some noise, and as a result she heard him

g) A superlative or adjectives like **premier** (first), **dernier** (last), **seul** (only) followed by **qui** or **que**:

c'était le coureur le plus rapide que j'aie jamais vu
he was the fastest runner I ever saw

Note, however, that the indicative is used with a statement of fact rather than the expression of an opinion:

c'est lui qui me l'a dit
it was he who told me

h) Negative and indefinite pronouns (eg **rien, personne, quelqu'un**) followed by **qui** or **que**:

je ne connais personne qui fasse aussi bien les crêpes
I don't know anyone who can make such good crêpes

il n'y a aucune chance qu'il réussisse
he hasn't got a chance of succeeding

ils cherchent quelqu'un qui puisse garder le bébé
they're looking for someone who can look after the baby

Note, however, that the subjunctive is not used if the verbs in both clauses have the same subject. The infinitive will be used in the subordinate clause instead, sometimes introduced by a preposition (**à** or **de**) (see pp 146-52).

a) de + infinitive replaces the subjunctive after:

  i) verbs of emotion:

    j'ai été étonné d'apprendre la nouvelle
    I was surprised to hear the news

    il regrette de ne pas être arrivé plus tôt
    he's sorry he didn't arrive earlier

    tu as peur de ne pas avoir assez d'argent?
    are you worried you won't have enough money?

  ii) **attendre** (to wait) and **douter** (to doubt):

    j'attendrai d'avoir bu mon café
    I'll wait until I've drunk my coffee

  iii) most impersonal constructions:

    il serait préférable de les en informer tout de suite
    it would be better to let them know immediately

    il est indispensable de parler une langue étrangère
    it's essential to be able to speak a foreign language

  iv) most conjunctions:

    il est resté dans la voiture afin de ne pas se mouiller
    he stayed in the car so as not to get wet

    j'ai lu avant de m'endormir
    I read before falling asleep

    tu peux sortir à condition de rentrer avant minuit
    you can go out, as long as you're back before midnight

b) à + infinitive replaces the subjunctive after:

  i) **de façon/manière**

    mets la liste sur la table de manière à ne pas l'oublier
    put the list on the table so that you won't forget it

  ii) **premier, seul, dernier**

    il a été le seul à s'excuser
    he was the only one who apologized

c) The infinitive without any linking preposition replaces the subjunctive after:

i) verbs of wishing and willing:

je voudrais sortir avec toi
I'd like to go out with you

ii) **il faut, il vaut mieux**:

il vous faudra prendre des chèques de voyage
you'll have to take some traveller's cheques

il lui a fallu recommencer à zéro
he had to start all over again

il vaudrait mieux lui apporter des fleurs que des bonbons
it would be better to take her flowers than sweets

Note that **il faut** + infinitive is used to state a generality. If one particular person etc is the subject of the action, an indirect object is used:

il faut réserver à l'avance
you have to book in advance

il lui faut se dépêcher
he has to hurry

iii) verbs of thinking:

je ne crois pas le connaître
I don't think I know him

tu penses être chez toi à cinq heures?
do you think you'll be home at five?

iv) **pour** and **sans**:

le car est reparti sans nous attendre
the coach left without waiting for us

j'économise pour pouvoir acheter une moto
I'm saving up to buy a motorbike

2. THE CONDITIONAL

a) The conditional present

i) The conditional present is used to describe what someone would do or would be doing, or what would happen (if something else were to happen):

si j'avais de l'argent, je ferais le tour du monde
if I had money, I would travel around the world

Note that when the main verb is in the conditional present, the verb after **si** is in the imperfect.

ii) It is also used in indirect questions or reported speech instead of the future:

il ne m'a pas dit s'il *viendrait*
he didn't tell me whether he *would come*

b) The conditional perfect (or past conditional)

The conditional perfect or past conditional is used to express what someone would have done or would have been doing or what would have happened:

si j'avais su, je n'aurais rien dit
if I had known, I wouldn't have said anything

qu'aurais-je fait sans toi?
what would I have done without you?

Note that if the main verb is in the conditional perfect, the verb introduced by **si** is in the pluperfect.

c) Tenses after **si**:

The tense of the verb introduced by **si** is determined by the tense of the verb in the main clause:

MAIN VERB		VERB FOLLOWING 'SI'
conditional present	→	imperfect
conditional perfect	→	pluperfect

> **je te le dirais si je le savais**
> I would tell you if I knew

> **je te l'aurais dit si je l'avais su**
> I would have told you if I had known

The conditional and the future should never be used with **si** unless **si** means 'whether' (ie when it introduces an indirect question):

> **je me demande si j'y serais arrivé sans toi**
> I wonder if I would have managed without you

3. THE IMPERATIVE

a) *Definition*

The imperative is used to give commands or polite instructions, or to make requests or suggestions; these can be positive ('do!') or negative ('don't!'):

> **mange ta soupe!**
> eat your soup!

> **n'aie pas peur!**
> don't be afraid!

> **partons!**
> let's go!

> **entrez!**
> come in!

> **faites attention!**
> be careful!

> **n'hésitez pas!**
> don't hesitate!

> **tournez à droite à la poste**
> turn right at the post office

b) *Forms*

The imperative has only three forms, which are the same as the **tu**, **nous** and **vous** forms of the present tense, but without the subject pronoun:

	-**ER** VERBS	-**IR** VERBS	-**RE** VERBS
'tu' form:	**regarde** watch	**choisis** choose	**attends** wait
'nous' form:	**regardons** let's watch	**choisissons** let's choose	**attendons** let's wait

'vous' form:	**regardez**	**choisissez**	**attendez**
	watch	choose	wait

Note:

i) The **-s** of the **tu** form of **-er** verbs is dropped, except when **y** or **en** follow the verb:

parle-lui!	**parles-en avec lui**
speak to him!	speak to him about it

achète du sucre!	**achètes-en un kilo**
buy some sugar!	buy a kilo (of it)

ii) The distinction between the subject pronouns **tu** and **vous** (see p 70) applies to the **tu** and **vous** forms of the imperative:

prends ta sœur avec toi
take your sister with you

prenez le plat du jour, Monsieur; c'est du poulet rôti
have today's special, sir; it's roast chicken

ouvrez vos livres à la page 24
open your books at page 24

c) *Negative commands*

In negative commands, the verb is placed between **ne** and **pas** (or the second part of other negative expressions):

ne fais pas ça!	**ne dites rien!**
don't do that!	don't say anything!

d) *Imperative with object pronouns*

In positive commands, object pronouns come after the verb and are attached to it by a hyphen. In negative commands, they come before the verb (see pp 79-85):

dites-moi ce qui s'est passé	**attendons-les!**
tell me what happened	let's wait for them

prends-en bien soin, ne l'abîme pas!	
take good care of it, don't damage it!	

ne le leur dis pas!	**ne les écoutez pas**
don't tell them (that)!	don't listen to them

e) *Imperative of reflexive verbs*

The position of the reflexive pronoun of reflexive verbs is the same as that of object pronouns:

tais-toi!
be quiet!

levez-vous!
get up!

méfiez-vous de lui
don't trust him

arrêtons-nous ici
let's stop here

ne nous plaignons pas
let's not complain

ne t'approche pas plus!
don't come any closer!

f) *Alternatives to the imperative*

i) infinitive

the infinitive is often used instead of the imperative in written instructions and in recipes:

s'adresser au concierge
see the caretaker

ne pas fumer
no smoking

verser le lait et bien mélanger
pour in the milk and mix well

ii) subjunctive

as the imperative has no third person (singular or plural), **que** + subjunctive is used for giving orders in the third person:

que personne ne me dérange!
don't let anyone disturb me!

qu'il entre!
let him (come) in!

qu'elle parte, je m'en fiche!
I don't care if she goes!

g) *Idiomatic usage*

The imperative is used in spoken French in many set phrases. Here are some of the most common ones:

allons donc!
you don't say!
hey! *(protest)*

dis/dites donc!
by the way!

tiens/tenez!
here you are!

tiens (donc)!
(oh) really?

voyons!
come (on) now!

tiens! voilà le facteur
ah! here comes the postman

tiens! tiens!
well, well!

voyons donc!
let's see now

H. The Infinitive

1. The infinitive is the basic form of the verb. It is recognizable by its ending, which is found in three forms corresponding to the three conjugations: **-er, -ir, -re**.

These endings give the verb the meaning 'to …':

acheter	**choisir**	**vendre**
to buy	to choose	to sell

Note that although this applies as a general rule, the French infinitive will often be translated by a verbal construction ending in **-ing** (see pp 256-8).

2. Uses of the infinitive

The infinitive can follow a preposition, a verb, a noun, a pronoun, an adverb or an adjective.

a) *After a preposition*

The infinitive can be used after some prepositions (**pour, avant de, sans, au lieu de, afin de** etc):

sans attendre	**avant de partir**
without waiting	before leaving

b) *After a verb*

There are three main constructions when a verb is followed by an infinitive:

i) Verbs followed by the infinitive with no linking preposition:

◻ verbs of wishing and willing, eg:

vouloir	to want
souhaiter	to wish
désirer	to wish, to want
espérer	to hope

voulez-vous manger maintenant ou plus tard?
do you want to eat now or later?

je souhaite parler au directeur
I wish to speak to the manager

□ verbs of seeing, hearing and feeling, eg:

voir	to see
écouter	to listen to
regarder	to watch
sentir	to feel, to smell
entendre	to hear

je l'ai vu jouer
I've seen him play

tu m'as regardé danser?
did you watch me dance?

j'ai entendu quelqu'un crier
I heard someone shout

□ verbs of motion, eg:

aller	to go
monter	to go/come up
venir	to come
entrer	to go/come in
rentrer	to go/come home
sortir	to go/come out
descendre	to go/come down

je viendrai te voir demain
I'll come and see you tomorrow

il est descendu laver la voiture
he went down to wash the car

va acheter le journal
go and buy the paper

Note that in English, 'to come' and 'to go' may be linked to the verb that follows by 'and'; 'and' is not translated in French.

aller + infinitive can be used to express a future action:

qu'est-ce que tu vas faire demain?
what are you going to do tomorrow?

□ modal auxiliary verbs (see pp 163-6)

□ verbs of liking and disliking, eg:

aimer	to like
adorer	to love
aimer mieux	to prefer
détester	to hate
préférer	to prefer

tu aimes voyager?
do you like travelling?

je déteste aller à la campagne
I hate going to the country

j'adore faire la grasse matinée
I love having a lie-in

j'aime mieux attendre
I'd rather wait

□ some impersonal verbs (see p 122)

□ a few other verbs, eg:

compter	to intend to
sembler	to seem
laisser	to let, to allow
faillir	'to nearly' (do)
oser	to dare

ils l'ont laissé partir
they let him go

je n'ose pas le leur demander
I daren't ask them

tu sembles être malade
you seem to be ill

je compte partir demain
I intend to leave tomorrow

j'ai failli manquer l'avion
I nearly missed the plane

□ in the following set expressions:

aller chercher	to go and get, to fetch
envoyer chercher	to send for
entendre dire (que)	to hear (that)

entendre parler de	to hear about
laisser tomber	to drop
venir chercher	to come and get
vouloir dire	to mean

va chercher ton argent
go and get your money

j'ai entendu dire qu'il était journaliste
I've heard that he's a journalist

tu as entendu parler de ce film?
have you heard about this film?

ne le laisse pas tomber!
don't drop it!

ça veut dire 'demain'
it means 'tomorrow'

ii) Verbs followed by **à** + infinitive

A list of these is given on p 201:

je dois aider ma mère à préparer le déjeuner
I must help my mother prepare lunch

il commence à faire nuit
it's beginning to get dark

alors, tu t'es décidé à y aller?
so you've made up your mind to go?

je t'invite à venir chez moi pour les vacances de Noël
you are welcome to come to my house for the Christmas holidays

je passe mon temps à lire et à regarder la télé
I spend my time reading and watching TV

cela sert à ouvrir les bouteilles
this is used for opening bottles

iii) Verbs followed by **de** + infinitive

A list of these is given on pp 202-3:

je crois qu'il s'est arrêté de pleuvoir
I think it's stopped raining

tu as envie de sortir?
do you feel like going out?

le médecin a conseillé à Serge de rester au lit
the doctor advised Serge to stay in bed

j'ai décidé de rester chez moi
I decided to stay at home

essayons de faire du stop
let's try and hitch-hike

demande à Papa de t'aider
ask Dad to help you

n'oublie pas d'en acheter!
don't forget to buy some!

je vous prie de m'excuser
please forgive me

tu as fini de m'ennuyer?
will you stop annoying me?

je t'interdis d'y aller
I forbid you to go

j'ai refusé de le faire
I refused to do it

il vient de téléphoner
he's just phoned

c) *After a noun, a pronoun, an adverb or an adjective*

There are two possible constructions:

i) with the linking preposition **à**:

il avait plusieurs clients à voir
he had several customers to see

c'est difficile à dire
it's difficult to say

une maison à vendre
a house for sale

j'ai des examens à préparer
I've got exams to prepare

il nous a indiqué la route à suivre
he showed us the road to follow

il n'y a pas de temps à perdre
there's no time to lose

c'était une occasion à ne pas manquer
it was an opportunity not to be missed

□ **à** conveys the idea of something to do or to be done after the following:

beaucoup	a lot
plus	more
tant	so much
trop	too much
assez	enough
moins	less
rien	nothing
tout	everything
quelque chose	something

il y a trop de livres à lire
there are too many books to read

il n'y a rien à ajouter
there's nothing further to add

elle a quelque chose à nous annoncer
she has something to tell us

□ **à** is used in a passive sense (when something is being done) and after **c'est**:

un livre agréable à lire
a pleasant book to read

il est facile à satisfaire
he is easily satisfied

c'est intéressant à savoir
that's interesting to know

c'était impossible à faire
it was impossible to do

ii) with the linking preposition **de**:

je suis content de te voir
I am pleased to see you

❑ **de** is used after nouns of an abstract nature, usually with the definite article, eg:

l'habitude de	the habit of
l'occasion de	the opportunity to
le temps de	the time to
le courage de	the courage to
l'envie de	the desire to
le besoin de	the need to
le plaisir de	the pleasure of
le moment de	the time to

il n'avait pas l'habitude d'être seul
he wasn't used to being alone

je n'ai pas le temps de leur expliquer
I don't have time to explain it to them

avez-vous eu l'occasion de la rencontrer?
did you have the opportunity to meet her?

ce n'est pas le moment de le déranger
now is not the time to disturb him

je n'ai pas eu le courage de te le dire
I didn't have the courage to tell you

❑ **de** is used after **il est** in an impersonal sense (see p 114):

il est intéressant de savoir que …
it is interesting to know that …

For information on the use of **c'est** and **il est**, see pp 258-9.

❑ **de** is used after many adjectives, and is frequently used to translate 'of' in English, eg:

certain/sûr de	certain of/to
capable de	capable of
incapable de	incapable of
coupable de	guilty of

j'étais sûr de réussir
I was sure of succeeding

il est incapable d'y arriver seul
he is incapable of managing on his own

◻ **de** is also used with adjectives relating to emotions and states of
mind, eg:

content de	pleased/happy to
surpris/étonné de	surprised to
fier de	proud to
heureux de	happy to
fâché de	annoyed to/at
triste de	sad to
gêné de	embarrassed to
désolé de	sorry for/to

j'ai été très content de recevoir ta lettre
I was very pleased to get your letter

elle sera surprise de vous voir
she will be surprised to see you

nous avons été très tristes d'apprendre la nouvelle
we were very sad to hear the news

Note, however, that **à** is used with **prêt à** (ready to) and **disposé à**
(willing to):

es-tu prêt à partir?
are you ready to go?

je suis tout disposé à vous aider
I'm very willing to help you

d) *faire* + infinitive

faire is followed by an infinitive without any linking preposition to
express the sense of 'having someone do something' or 'having
something done'; two constructions are possible, depending on
whether there are one or two objects:

i) when only one object is used, it is a direct object:

je dois le faire réparer
I must have it fixed

il veut faire repeindre sa voiture
he wants to have his car resprayed

153

cette veste est sale, il faut la faire nettoyer
this jacket's dirty, I'll have to have it cleaned

tu m'as fait attendre!
you kept me waiting!

je le ferai parler
I'll make him talk

Note the following set expressions:

faire entrer	to show in
faire venir	to send for

faites entrer ce monsieur
show this gentleman in

je vais faire venir le docteur
I'll send for the doctor

ii) when both **faire** and the following infinitive have an object, the object of **faire** is indirect:

elle m'a fait prendre une douche
she made me take a shower

je leur ai fait ranger leur chambre
I made them tidy their room

e) *Infinitive used as subject of another verb:*

trouver un emploi n'est pas facile
finding a job isn't easy

devenir pilote était mon rêve
my dream was to become a pilot

3. The perfect infinitive

a) *Form*

The perfect or past infinitive is formed with the infinitive of the auxiliary **avoir** or **être** as appropriate (see pp 112-17), followed by the past participle of the verb, eg:

avoir mangé	**être allé**	**s'être levé**
to have eaten	to have gone	to have got up

b) *Use*

i) after the preposition **après** (after):

après avoir attendu une heure, il est rentré chez lui
after waiting for an hour, he went back home

j'ai compris la remarque après avoir relu le livre
I understood the remark after reading the book again

ii) after certain verbs:

se souvenir de	to remember
remercier de	to thank for
regretter de	to regret, to be sorry for
être désolé de	to be sorry for

je vous remercie de m'avoir invité
thank you for inviting me

il regrettait de leur avoir menti
he was sorry he had lied to them

tu te souviens d'avoir fait cela?
do you remember doing this?

I. Participles

1. The present participle

a) *Formation*

Like the imperfect, the present participle is formed by using the stem of the first person plural of the present tense (the **nous** form without the **-ons** ending) to which **ant** (like English **ing**) is added. The following three verbs, however, have irregular present participles:

INFINITIVE	PRESENT PARTICIPLE
avoir to have	**ayant** having
être to be	**étant** being
savoir to know	**sachant** knowing

b) *Use as an adjective*

Used as an adjective, the present participle agrees in number and in gender with its noun or pronoun:

un travail fatigant
tiring work

la semaine suivante
the following week

ils sont très exigeants
they're very demanding

des nouvelles surprenantes
surprising news

c) *Use as a verb*

The present participle is used far less frequently in French than in English, and English present participles in **-ing** are often not translated by a participle in French (see pp 256-8).

i) Used on its own, the present participle corresponds to the English present participle:

ne voulant plus attendre, ils sont partis sans moi
not wanting to wait any longer, they left without me

pensant bien faire, j'ai insisté
thinking I was doing the right thing, I insisted

ii) **en** + present participle

When the subject of the present participle is the same as that of the main verb, this structure is often used to express simultaneous actions (ie 'while doing something'), manner (ie 'by doing something') and to translate English phrasal verbs expressing motion.

▫ simultaneous actions

In English this structure is translated by:

> while/when/on + present participle (eg 'on arriving')
> while/when/as + subject + verb (eg 'as he arrived')

> **il est tombé en descendant l'escalier**
> he fell as he was going down the stairs

> **en le voyant, j'ai éclaté de rire**
> when I saw him, I burst out laughing

> **elle lisait le journal en attendant l'autobus**
> she was reading the paper while waiting for the bus

Note that the adverb **tout** is often used before **en** to emphasize the fact that the actions are simultaneous, especially when there is an element of contradiction:

> **elle écoutait la radio tout en faisant ses devoirs**
> she was listening to the radio while doing her homework

> **tout en protestant, je les ai suivis**
> under protest, I followed them

▫ manner

When expressing how an action is done, **en** + participle is translated by 'by' + participle, eg:

> **il gagne sa vie en vendant des voitures d'occasion**
> he earns his living (by) selling second-hand cars

> **j'ai trouvé du travail en lisant les petites annonces**
> I found a job by reading the classified ads

▫ phrasal verbs of motion

en + present participle is often used to translate English phrasal verbs expressing motion, where the verb expresses the means of motion and a preposition expresses the direction of movement (eg 'to run out', 'to swim across').

In French, the English preposition is translated by a verb, while the English verb is translated by **en** + present participle.

il est sorti du magasin *en courant*
he *ran* out of the shop

elle a traversé la route *en titubant*
she *staggered* across the road

2. The past participle

a) *Forms*

For the formation of the past participle see p 112.

b) *Use*

The past participle is mostly used as a verb in compound tenses or in the passive, but it can also be used as an adjective. In either case, there are strict rules of agreement to be followed.

i) When it is used as an adjective, the past participle always agrees with the noun or pronoun to which it refers:

un pneu crevé a burst tyre	**une pomme pourrie** a rotten apple
ils étaient épuisés they were exhausted	**des photos prises à la nuit tombée** photos taken at nightfall

Note that in French, the past participle is used as an adjective to describe postures or attitudes of the body, where English uses the present participle. The most common of these are:

accoudé	leaning on one's elbows
accroupi	squatting
agenouillé	kneeling
allongé	lying (down)
appuyé (contre)	leaning (against)
couché	lying (down)
étendu	lying (down)
penché	leaning (over)
(sus)pendu	hanging

il est allongé sur le lit
he's lying on the bed

une femme assise devant moi
a woman sitting in front of me

ii) In compound tenses:

□ With the auxiliary **avoir** the past participle agrees in number and gender with the direct object only when the direct object comes before the participle, ie in the following cases:

in a clause introduced by the relative pronoun **que**:

le jeu vidéo que j'ai acheté
the video game I bought

la valise qu'il a perdue
the suitcase he lost

with a direct object pronoun:

je ne trouve pas la disquette; où l'as-tu mise?
I can't find the floppy disk; where did you put it?

merci pour tes suggestions, je les ai trouvées très utiles
thank you for your suggestions; I found them very useful

in a clause introduced by **combien de, quel** or **lequel**:

combien de pays as-tu visités?
how many countries have you visited?

laquelle avez-vous choisie?
which one did you choose?

Note that if the direct object comes after the past participle, the participle remains in the masculine singular form:

on a rencontré des gens très sympathiques
we met some very nice people

□ With the auxiliary **être** the past participle agrees with the subject of the verb:

quand est-elle revenue?
when did she come back?

elle était déjà partie
she'd already left

ils sont passés te voir?
did they come to see you?

elles sont restées là
they stayed here

Note that this rule also applies when the verb is in the passive:

elle a été arrêtée
she's been arrested

▫ With reflexive verbs the past participle normally agrees with the reflexive pronoun if the pronoun is a direct object; since the reflexive pronoun refers to the subject, the number and gender of the past participle are determined by the subject:

Jacques s'est trompé
Jacques made a mistake

Marie s'était levée tard
Marie had got up late

ils se sont disputés?
did they have an argument?

elles se sont vues
they saw each other

Michèle et Marie, vous vous êtes habillées?
Michèle and Marie, have you got dressed yet?

Note, however, that the past participle does not agree when the reflexive pronoun is an indirect object:

elles se sont écrit
they wrote *to* each other

elle s'est lavé les cheveux
she washed her hair

ils se sont serré la main
they shook hands

J. The Passive

1. Formation

The passive is used when the subject does not perform the action, but is subjected to it, eg:

the house has been sold   he was made redundant

Passive tenses are formed with the corresponding tense of the verb **'être'** ('to be', as in English), followed by the past participle of the verb, eg:

j'ai été invité
I was invited

The past participle must agree with its subject, eg:

il sera puni   **elle a été renvoyée**
he will be punished   she has been dismissed

ils seront déçus   **elles ont été vues**
they will be disappointed   they were seen

2. Avoidance of the passive

The passive is far less common in French than in English. In particular, an indirect object cannot become the subject of a sentence in French; the following sentence, where 'he' is an indirect object, has no equivalent in French:

he was given a book *(ie a book was given to him)*

In general, French tries to avoid the passive wherever possible. This can be done in several ways.

a) *By using the pronoun* **on**:

on m'a volé mon portefeuille
my wallet has been stolen

on construit une nouvelle piscine
a new swimming pool is being built

en France, on boit beaucoup de vin
a lot of wine is drunk in France

b) *By making the agent the subject of the verb*

If the agent, that is the real subject, is mentioned in English, it can become the subject of the French verb:

> **la nouvelle va les surprendre**
> they will be surprised by *the news*

> **mon correspondant m'a invité**
> I've been invited by *my penfriend*

> **mon cadeau te plaît?**
> are you pleased with *my present*?

c) *By using a reflexive verb*

Reflexive forms can be created for a large number of verbs, particularly in the third person:

> **elle s'appelle Anne**
> she is called Anne

> **ton absence va se remarquer**
> your absence will be noticed

> **ce plat se mange froid**
> this dish is eaten cold

> **cela ne se fait pas ici**
> that isn't done here

d) *By using **se faire** + infinitive (when the subject is a person)*

> **il s'est fait renverser par une voiture**
> he was run over by a car

> **je me suis fait couper les cheveux**
> I've had my hair cut

3. Conjugation

For the complete conjugation of a verb in the passive, see **être aimé** (to be loved) p 170.

K. Modal Auxiliary Verbs

The modal auxiliary verbs are always followed by the infinitive. They express an obligation, a probability, an intention, a possibility or a wish rather than a fact.

The five modal auxiliary verbs are: **devoir, pouvoir, savoir, vouloir**, and **falloir**.

1. Devoir (for conjugation see p 178) is used to express the following:

a) *obligation*

nous devons arriver à temps we must arrive in time	**nous avions dû partir** we had (had) to go
demain tu devras prendre le bus tomorrow you'll have to take the bus	**j'ai dû avouer que j'avais tort** I had to admit that I was wrong

In the conditional, **devoir** may be used for advice, ie to express what should be done (conditional present) or should have been done (conditional past):

vous devriez travailler davantage
you ought to/should work harder

tu ne devrais pas marcher sur l'herbe
you shouldn't walk on the grass

tu aurais dû tout avouer
you should have admitted everything

tu n'aurais pas dû manger ces champignons
you shouldn't have eaten those mushrooms

Note that the French infinitive is translated by a past participle in English: **manger** = eaten.

b) *probability*

il doit être en train de dormir
he must be sleeping (he's probably sleeping)

163

j'ai dû me tromper de chemin
I must have taken the wrong road

Note that in a past narrative sequence in the distant past, 'must have' is translated by a pluperfect in French:

il dit qu'il avait dû se tromper de chemin
he said he must have taken the wrong road

c) *intention, expectation*

je dois aller chez le dentiste
I am supposed to go to the dentist

le train doit arriver à 19h30
the train is due to arrive at 7.30p.m.

2. Pouvoir (for conjugation see p 190) is used to express the following:

a) *capacity/ability*

il peut rester plusieurs jours sans dormir
he can go without sleep for several days

cette voiture peut faire du 150
this car can go up to 93 mph

il était si faible qu'il ne pouvait pas sortir de son lit
he was so weak that he couldn't get out of bed

b) *permission*

puis-je entrer?
may I come in?

puis-je vous offrir du thé?
may I offer you some tea?

c) *possibility*

cela peut arriver
it can happen

ça peut n'avoir aucune importance
it might not be at all important

Note that **pouvoir** + the infinitive is usually replaced by **peut-être** + the finite tense, eg **il s'est peut-être trompé de livres** (he may have taken the wrong books).

In the conditional, **pouvoir** is used to express something that could or might be (conditional present) or that could or might have been (conditional past):

> **tu pourrais t'excuser**
> you might apologize

> **j'aurais pu vous prêter mon téléphone portable**
> I could have lent you my mobile phone

Note that with verbs of perception, eg **entendre** (to hear), **sentir** (to feel, to smell), **voir** (to see), **pouvoir** is often omitted.

> **j'entendais le bruit des vagues**
> I could hear the sound of the waves

3. Savoir (for conjugation see p 193) is used to express 'to know how to':

> **je sais/savais conduire une moto**
> I can/used to be able to ride a motorbike

> **elle sait parler plusieurs langues**
> she can speak several languages

4. Vouloir (for conjugation see p 199) is used to express the following:

a) *desire*

> **je veux partir**
> I want to go

> **voulez-vous danser avec moi?**
> will you dance with me?

b) *wish*

> **je voudrais être riche**
> I wish I were rich

> **je voudrais trouver un travail intéressant**
> I'd like to find an interesting job

> **j'aurais voulu te donner un coup de poing**
> I would have liked to punch you

c) *intention*

> **il a voulu sauter par la fenêtre**
> he tried to jump out of the window

Note that **veuillez**, the imperative of **vouloir**, is used as a polite form to express a request ('would you please …'):

veuillez ne pas déranger
please do not disturb

5. Falloir (for conjugation see p 185) is used to express necessity:

il faut manger pour vivre
you must eat to live

il faudrait y aller tout de suite
we should go right away

il aurait fallu apporter des sandwichs
we should have brought sandwiches

Note that some of the above verbs can also be used without infinitive constructions in which case they have a different meaning, eg **devoir** = to owe, **savoir** = to know.

je te dois 20 euros
I owe you 20 euros

elle le sait par cœur
she knows it by heart

L. Conjugation Tables

The following verbs provide the main patterns of conjugation including the conjugation of the most common irregular verbs. They are arranged in alphabetical order:

-er verb *(see p 100)*	AIMER
-ir verb *(see p 100)*	FINIR
-re verb *(see p 100)*	VENDRE
Reflexive verb *(see pp 118-21)*	SE MÉFIER
Verb with auxiliary **être** *(see pp 114-7)*	ARRIVER
Verb in the passive *(see pp 161-2)*	ÊTRE AIMÉ
Auxiliaries *(see pp 112-7)*	AVOIR
	ÊTRE
Verb in **-eler/-eter** *(see pp 106-7)*	APPELER
Verb in **-e** + consonant + **er** *(see pp 109)*	ACHETER
Verb in **é** + consonant + **er** *(see pp 110-11)*	ESPÉRER
Modal auxiliaries *(see pp 163-6)*	DEVOIR
	POUVOIR
	SAVOIR
	VOULOIR
	FALLOIR

Irregular verbs		
	ALLER	METTRE
	CONDUIRE	OUVRIR
	CONNAÎTRE	PRENDRE
	CROIRE	RECEVOIR
	DIRE	TENIR
	DORMIR	VENIR
	ÉCRIRE	VIVRE
	FAIRE	VOIR

'Harrap French Verbs', a fully comprehensive list of French verbs and their conjugations, is also available in this series.

ACHETER   to buy

PRESENT	IMPERFECT	FUTURE
j'achète	j'achetais	j'achèterai
tu achètes	tu achetais	tu achèteras
il achète	il achetait	il achètera
nous achetons	nous achetions	nous achèterons
vous achetez	vous achetiez	vous achèterez
ils achètent	ils achetaient	ils achèteront

PAST HISTORIC	PERFECT	PLUPERFECT
j'achetai	j'ai acheté	j'avais acheté
tu achetas	tu as acheté	tu avais acheté
il acheta	il a acheté	il avait acheté
nous achetâmes	nous avons acheté	nous avions acheté
vous achetâtes	vous avez acheté	vous aviez acheté
ils achetèrent	ils ont acheté	ils avaient acheté

CONDITIONAL

PAST ANTERIOR	PRESENT	PAST
j'eus acheté etc	j'achèterais	j'aurais acheté
	tu achèterais	tu aurais acheté
	il achèterait	il aurait acheté
	nous achèterions	nous aurions acheté
FUTURE PERFECT	vous achèteriez	vous auriez acheté
j'aurai acheté etc	ils achèteraient	ils auraient acheté

SUBJUNCTIVE

PRESENT	IMPERFECT	PERFECT
j'achète	j'achetasse	j'aie acheté
tu achètes	tu achetasses	tu aies acheté
il achète	il achetât	il ait acheté
nous achetions	nous achetassions	nous ayons acheté
vous achetiez	vous achetassiez	vous ayez acheté
ils achètent	ils achetassent	ils aient acheté

IMPERATIVE	INFINITIVE	PARTICIPLE
achète	**PRESENT**	**PRESENT**
achetons	acheter	achetant
achetez		
	PAST	**PAST**
	avoir acheté	acheté

AIMER   to like/to love

PRESENT	IMPERFECT	FUTURE
j'aime	j'aimais	j'aimerai
tu aimes	tu aimais	tu aimeras
il aime	il aimait	il aimera
nous aimons	nous aimions	nous aimerons
vous aimez	vous aimiez	vous aimerez
ils aiment	ils aimaient	ils aimeront

PAST HISTORIC	PERFECT	PLUPERFECT
j'aimai	j'ai aimé	j'avais aimé
tu aimas	tu as aimé	tu avais aimé
il aima	il a aimé	il avait aimé
nous aimâmes	nous avons aimé	nous avions aimé
vous aimâtes	vous avez aimé	vous aviez aimé
ils aimèrent	ils ont aimé	ils avaient aimé

CONDITIONAL

PAST ANTERIOR	PRESENT	PAST
j'eus aimé etc	j'aimerais	j'aurais aimé
	tu aimerais	tu aurais aimé
	il aimerait	il aurait aimé
	nous aimerions	nous aurions aimé
FUTURE PERFECT	vous aimeriez	vous auriez aimé
j'aurai aimé etc	ils aimeraient	ils auraient aimé

SUBJUNCTIVE

PRESENT	IMPERFECT	PERFECT
j'aime	j'aimasse	j'aie aimé
tu aimes	tu aimasses	tu aies aimé
il aime	il aimât	il ait aimé
nous aimions	nous aimassions	nous ayons aimé
vous aimiez	vous aimassiez	vous ayez aimé
ils aiment	ils aimassent	ils aient aimé

IMPERATIVE	INFINITIVE	PARTICIPLE
aime	**PRESENT**	**PRESENT**
aimons	aimer	aimant
aimez		
	PAST	**PAST**
	avoir aimé	aimé

ÊTRE AIMÉ to be loved

PRESENT	IMPERFECT	FUTURE
je suis aimé(e)	j'étais aimé(e)	je serai aimé(e)
tu es aimé(e)	tu étais aimé(e)	tu seras aimé(e)
il (elle) est aimé(e)	il (elle) était aimé(e)	il (elle) sera aimé(e)
nous sommes aimé(e)s	nous étions aimé(e)s	nous serons aimé(e)s
vous êtes aimé(e)(s)	vous étiez aimé(e)(s)	vous serez aimé(e)(s)
ils (elles) sont aimé(e)s	ils (elles) étaient aimé(e)s	ils seront aimé(e)s

PAST HISTORIC	PERFECT	PLUPERFECT
je fus aimé(e)	j'ai été aimé(e)	j'avais été aimé(e)
tu fus aimé(e)	tu as été aimé(e)	tu avais été aimé(e)
il (elle) fut aimé(e)	il (elle) a été aimé(e)	il (elle) avait été aimé(e)
nous fûmes aimé(e)s	nous avons été aimé(e)s	nous avions été aimé(e)s
vous fûtes aimé(e)(s)	vous avez été aimé(e)(s)	vous aviez été aimé(e)(s)
ils (elles) furent aimé(e)s	ils (elles) ont été aimé(e)s	ils (elles) avaient été aimé(e)s

CONDITIONAL

PAST ANTERIOR	PRESENT	PAST
j'eus été aimé(e) etc	je serais aimé(e)	j'aurais été aimé(e)
	tu serais aimé(e)	tu aurais été aimé(e)
	il (elle) serait aimé(e)	il (elle) aurait été aimé(e)
	nous serions aimé(e)s	nous aurions été aimé(e)s
FUTURE PERFECT	vous seriez aimé(e)(s)	vous auriez été aimé(e)(s)
j'aurai été aimé(e) etc	ils (elles) seraient aimé(e)s	ils (elles) auraient été aimé(e)s

SUBJUNCTIVE

PRESENT	IMPERFECT	PERFECT
je sois aimé(e)	je fusse aimé(e)	j'aie été aimé(e)
tu sois aimé(e)	tu fusses aimé(e)	tu aies été aimé(e)
il (elle) soit aimé(e)	il (elle) fût aimé(e)	il (elle) ait été aimé(e)
nous soyons aimé(e)s	nous fussions aimé(e)s	nous ayons été aimé(e)s
vous soyez aimé(e)(s)	vous fussiez aimé(e)(s)	vous ayez été aimé(e)(s)
ils (elles) soient aimé(e)s	ils (elles) fussent aimé(e)s	ils (elles) aient été aimé(e)s

IMPERATIVE	INFINITIVE	PARTICIPLE
sois aimé(e)	PRESENT	PRESENT
soyons aimé(e)s	être aimé(e)(s)	étant aimé(e)(s)
soyez aimé(e)(s)		
	PAST	PAST
	avoir été aimé(e)(s)	été aimé(e)(s)

ALLER   to go

PRESENT	IMPERFECT	FUTURE
je vais	j'allais	j'irai
tu vas	tu allais	tu iras
il va	il allait	il ira
nous allons	nous allions	nous irons
vous allez	vous alliez	vous irez
ils vont	ils allaient	ils iront

PAST HISTORIC	PERFECT	PLUPERFECT
j'allai	je suis allé(e)	j'étais allé(e)
tu allas	tu es allé(e)	tu étais allé(e)
il alla	il (elle) est allé(e)	il (elle) était allé(e)
nous allâmes	nous sommes allé(e)s	nous étions allé(e)s
vous allâtes	vous êtes allé(e)(s)	vous étiez allé(e)(s)
ils allèrent	ils (elles) sont allé(e)s	ils (elles) étaient allé(e)s

CONDITIONAL

PAST ANTERIOR	PRESENT	PAST
je fus allé(e) etc	j'irais	je serais allé(e)
	tu irais	tu serais allé(e)
	il irait	il (elle) serait allé(e)
	nous irions	nous serions allé(e)s
FUTURE PERFECT	vous iriez	vous seriez allé(e)(s)
je serai allé(e) etc	ils iraient	ils (elles) seraient allé(e)s

SUBJUNCTIVE

PRESENT	IMPERFECT	PERFECT
j'aille	j'allasse	je sois allé(e)
tu ailles	tu allasses	tu sois allé(e)
il aille	il allât	il (elle) soit allé(e)
nous allions	nous allassions	nous soyons allé(e)s
vous alliez	vous allassiez	vous soyez allé(e)(s)
ils aillent	ils allassent	ils (elles) soient allé(e)s

IMPERATIVE	INFINITIVE	PARTICIPLE
va	**PRESENT**	**PRESENT**
allons	aller	allant
allez		
	PAST	**PAST**
	être allé(e)(s)	allé

APPELER to call

PRESENT	IMPERFECT	FUTURE
j'appelle	j'appelais	j'appellerai
tu appelles	tu appelais	tu appelleras
il appelle	il appelait	il appellera
nous appelons	nous appelions	nous appellerons
vous appelez	vous appeliez	vous appellerez
ils appellent	ils appelaient	ils appelleront

PAST HISTORIC	PERFECT	PLUPERFECT
j'appelai	j'ai appelé	j'avais appelé
tu appelas	tu as appelé	tu avais appelé
il appela	il a appelé	il avait appelé
nous appelâmes	nous avons appelé	nous avions appelé
vous appelâtes	vous avez appelé	vous aviez appelé
ils appelèrent	ils ont appelé	ils avaient appelé

CONDITIONAL

PAST ANTERIOR	PRESENT	PAST
j'eus appelé etc	j'appellerais	j'aurais appelé
	tu appellerais	tu aurais appelé
	il appellerait	il aurait appelé
	nous appellerions	nous aurions appelé
FUTURE PERFECT	vous appelleriez	vous auriez appelé
j'aurai appelé etc	ils appelleraient	ils auraient appelé

SUBJUNCTIVE

PRESENT	IMPERFECT	PERFECT
j'appelle	j'appelasse	j'aie appelé
tu appelles	tu appelasses	tu aies appelé
il appelle	il appelât	il ait appelé
nous appelions	nous appelassions	nous ayons appelé
vous appeliez	vous appelassiez	vous ayez appelé
ils appellent	ils appelassent	ils aient appelé

IMPERATIVE	INFINITIVE	PARTICIPLE
appelle	**PRESENT**	**PRESENT**
appelons	appeler	appelant
appelez		
	PAST	**PAST**
	avoir appelé	appelé

ARRIVER   to arrive/to happen

PRESENT	IMPERFECT	FUTURE
j'arrive	j'arrivais	j'arriverai
tu arrives	tu arrivais	tu arriveras
il arrive	il arrivait	il arrivera
nous arrivons	nous arrivions	nous arriverons
vous arrivez	vous arriviez	vous arriverez
ils arrivent	ils arrivaient	ils arriveront

PAST HISTORIC	PERFECT	PLUPERFECT
j'arrivai	je suis arrivé(e)	j'étais arrivé(e)
tu arrivas	tu es arrivé(e)	tu étais arrivé(e)
il arriva	il (elle) est arrivé(e)	il (elle) était arrivé(e)
nous arrivâmes	nous sommes arrivé(e)s	nous étions arrivé(e)s
vous arrivâtes	vous êtes arrivé(e)(s)	vous étiez arrivé(e)(s)
ils arrivèrent	ils (elles) sont arrivé(e)s	ils (elles) étaient arrivé(e)s

CONDITIONAL

PAST ANTERIOR	PRESENT	PAST
je fus arrivé(e) etc	j'arriverais	je serais arrivé(e)
	tu arriverais	tu serais arrivé(e)
	il arriverait	il (elle) serait arrivé(e)
FUTURE PERFECT	nous arriverions	nous serions arrivé(e)s
	vous arriveriez	vous seriez arrivé(e)(s)
je serai arrivé(e) etc	ils arriveraient	ils (elles) seraient arrivé(e)s

SUBJUNCTIVE

PRESENT	IMPERFECT	PERFECT
j'arrive	j'arrivasse	je sois arrivé(e)
tu arrives	tu arrivasses	tu sois arrivé(e)
il arrive	il arrivât	il (elle) soit arrivé(e)
nous arrivions	nous arrivassions	nous soyons arrivé(e)s
vous arriviez	vous arrivassiez	vous soyez arrivé(e)(s)
ils arrivent	ils arrivassent	ils (elles) soient arrivé(e)s

IMPERATIVE	INFINITIVE	PARTICIPLE
arrive	**PRESENT**	**PRESENT**
arrivons	arriver	arrivant
arrivez		
	PAST	**PAST**
	être arrivé(e)(s)	arrivé

AVOIR to have

PRESENT	IMPERFECT	FUTURE
j'ai	j'avais	j'aurai
tu as	tu avais	tu auras
il a	il avait	il aura
nous avons	nous avions	nous aurons
vous avez	vous aviez	vous aurez
ils ont	ils avaient	ils auront

PAST HISTORIC	PERFECT	PLUPERFECT
j'eus	j'ai eu	j'avais eu
tu eus	tu as eu	tu auras eu
il eut	il a eu	il avait eu
nous eûmes	nous avons eu	nous avions eu
vous eûtes	vous avez eu	vous aviez eu
ils eurent	ils ont eu	ils avaient eu

CONDITIONAL

PAST ANTERIOR	PRESENT	PAST
j'eus eu etc	j'aurais	j'aurais eu
	tu aurais	tu aurais eu
	il aurait	il aurait eu
	nous aurions	nous aurions eu
FUTURE PERFECT	vous auriez	vous auriez eu
j'aurai eu etc	ils auraient	ils auraient eu

SUBJUNCTIVE

PRESENT	IMPERFECT	PERFECT
j'aie	j'eusse	j'aie eu
tu aies	tu eusses	tu aies eu
il ait	il eût	il ait eu
nous ayons	nous eussions	nous ayons eu
vous ayez	vous eussiez	vous ayez eu
ils aient	ils eussent	ils aient eu

IMPERATIVE	INFINITIVE	PARTICIPLE
aie	**PRESENT**	**PRESENT**
ayons	avoir	ayant
ayez		
	PAST	**PAST**
	avoir eu	eu

CONDUIRE   to lead/to drive

PRESENT	IMPERFECT	FUTURE
je conduis	je conduisais	je conduirai
tu conduis	tu conduisais	tu conduiras
il conduit	il conduisait	il conduira
nous conduisons	nous conduisions	nous conduirons
vous conduisez	vous conduisiez	vous conduirez
ils conduisent	ils conduisaient	ils conduiront

PAST HISTORIC	PERFECT	PLUPERFECT
je conduisis	j'ai conduit	j'avais conduit
tu conduisis	tu as conduit	tu avais conduit
il conduisit	il a conduit	il avait conduit
nous conduisîmes	nous avons conduit	nous avions conduit
vous conduisîtes	vous avez conduit	vous aviez conduit
ils conduisirent	ils ont conduit	ils avaient conduit

CONDITIONAL

PAST ANTERIOR	PRESENT	PAST
j'eus conduit etc	je conduirais	j'aurais conduit
	tu conduirais	tu aurais conduit
	il conduirait	il aurait conduit
	nous conduirions	nous aurions conduit
FUTURE PERFECT	vous conduiriez	vous auriez conduit
j'aurai conduit etc	ils conduiraient	ils auraient conduit

SUBJUNCTIVE

PRESENT	IMPERFECT	PERFECT
je conduise	je conduisisse	j'aie conduit
tu conduises	tu conduisisses	tu aies conduit
il conduise	il conduisît	il ait conduit
nous conduisions	nous conduisissions	nous ayons conduit
vous conduisiez	vous conduisissiez	vous ayez conduit
ils conduisent	ils conduisissent	ils aient conduit

IMPERATIVE	INFINITIVE	PARTICIPLE
conduis	**PRESENT**	**PRESENT**
conduisons	conduire	conduisant
conduisez		
	PAST	**PAST**
	avoir conduit	conduit

CONNAÎTRE to know

PRESENT	**IMPERFECT**	**FUTURE**
je connais	je connaissais	je connaîtrai
tu connais	tu connaissais	tu connaîtras
il connaît	il connaissait	il connaîtra
nous connaissons	nous connaissions	nous connaîtrons
vous connaissez	vous connaissiez	vous connaîtrez
ils connaissent	ils connaissaient	ils connaîtront

PAST HISTORIC	**PERFECT**	**PLUPERFECT**
je connus	j'ai connu	j'avais connu
tu connus	tu as connu	tu avais connu
il connut	il a connu	il avait connu
nous connûmes	nous avons connu	nous avions connu
vous connûtes	vous avez connu	vous aviez connu
ils connurent	ils ont connu	ils avaient connu

CONDITIONAL

PAST ANTERIOR	**PRESENT**	**PAST**
j'eus connu etc	je connaîtrais	j'aurais connu
	tu connaîtrais	tu aurais connu
	il connaîtrait	il aurait connu
	nous connaîtrions	nous aurions connu
FUTURE PERFECT	vous connaîtriez	vous auriez connu
j'aurai connu etc	ils connaîtraient	ils auraient connu

SUBJUNCTIVE

PRESENT	**IMPERFECT**	**PERFECT**
je connaisse	je connusse	j'aie connu
tu connaisses	tu connusses	tu aies connu
il connaisse	il connût	il ait connu
nous connaissions	nous connussions	nous ayons connu
vous connaissiez	vous connussiez	vous ayez connu
ils connaissent	ils connussent	ils aient connu

IMPERATIVE	**INFINITIVE**	**PARTICIPLE**
	PRESENT	**PRESENT**
connais	connaître	connaissant
connaissons		
connaissez		
	PAST	**PAST**
	avoir connu	connu

CROIRE   to believe

PRESENT	IMPERFECT	FUTURE
je crois	je croyais	je croirai
tu crois	tu croyais	tu croiras
il croit	il croyait	il croira
nous croyons	nous croyions	nous croirons
vous croyez	vous croyiez	vous croirez
ils croient	ils croyaient	ils croiront

PAST HISTORIC	PERFECT	PLUPERFECT
je crus	j'ai cru	j'avais cru
tu crus	tu as cru	tu avais cru
il crut	il a cru	il avait cru
nous crûmes	nous avons cru	nous avions cru
vous crûtes	vous avez cru	vous aviez cru
ils crurent	ils ont cru	ils avaient cru

CONDITIONAL

PAST ANTERIOR	PRESENT	PAST
j'eus cru etc	je croirais	j'aurais cru
	tu croirais	tu aurais cru
	il croirait	il aurait cru
	nous croirions	nous aurions cru
FUTURE PERFECT	vous croiriez	vous auriez cru
j'aurai cru etc	ils croiraient	ils auraient cru

SUBJUNCTIVE

PRESENT	IMPERFECT	PERFECT
je croie	je crusse	j'aie cru
tu croies	tu crusses	tu aies cru
il croie	il crût	il ait cru
nous croyions	nous crussions	nous ayons cru
vous croyiez	vous crussiez	vous ayez cru
ils croient	ils crussent	ils aient cru

IMPERATIVE	INFINITIVE	PARTICIPLE
crois	**PRESENT**	**PRESENT**
croyons	croire	croyant
croyez		
	PAST	**PAST**
	avoir cru	cru

DEVOIR   to owe/to have to

PRESENT	IMPERFECT	FUTURE
je dois	je devais	je devrai
tu dois	tu devais	tu devras
il doit	il devait	il devra
nous devons	nous devions	nous devrons
vous devez	vous deviez	vous devrez
ils doivent	ils devaient	ils devront

PAST HISTORIC	PERFECT	PLUPERFECT
je dus	j'ai dû	j'avais dû
tu dus	tu as dû	tu avais dû
il dut	il a dû	il avait dû
nous dûmes	nous avons dû	nous avions dû
vous dûtes	vous avez dû	vous aviez dû
ils durent	ils ont dû	ils avaient dû

CONDITIONAL

PAST ANTERIOR	PRESENT	PAST
j'eus dû etc	je devrais	j'aurais dû
	tu devrais	tu aurais dû
	il devrait	il aurait dû
	nous devrions	nous aurions dû
FUTURE PERFECT	vous devriez	vous auriez dû
j'aurai dû	ils devraient	ils auraient dû

SUBJUNCTIVE

PRESENT	IMPERFECT	PERFECT
je doive	je dusse	j'aie dû
tu doives	tu dusses	tu aies dû
il doive	il dût	il ait dû
nous devions	nous dussions	nous ayons dû
vous deviez	vous dussiez	vous ayez dû
ils doivent	ils dussent	ils aient dû

IMPERATIVE	INFINITIVE	PARTICIPLE
dois	PRESENT	PRESENT
devons	devoir	devant
devez		
	PAST	PAST
	avoir dû	dû (due, dus)

DIRE   to say

PRESENT	IMPERFECT	FUTURE
je dis	je disais	je dirai
tu dis	tu disais	tu diras
il dit	il disait	il dira
nous disons	nous disions	nous dirons
vous dites	vous disiez	vous direz
ils disent	ils disaient	ils diront

PAST HISTORIC	PERFECT	PLUPERFECT
je dis	j'ai dit	j'avais dit
tu dis	tu as dit	tu avais dit
il dit	il a dit	il avait dit
nous dîmes	nous avons dit	nous avions dit
vous dîtes	vous avez dit	vous aviez dit
ils dirent	ils ont dit	ils avaient dit

CONDITIONAL

PAST ANTERIOR	PRESENT	PAST
j'eus dit etc	je dirais	j'aurais dit
	tu dirais	tu aurais dit
	il dirait	il aurait dit
	nous dirions	nous aurions dit
FUTURE PERFECT	vous diriez	vous auriez dit
j'aurai dit etc	ils diraient	ils auraient dit

SUBJUNCTIVE

PRESENT	IMPERFECT	PERFECT
je dise	je disse	j'aie dit
tu dises	tu disses	tu aies dit
il dise	il dît	il ait dit
nous disions	nous dissions	nous ayons dit
vous disiez	vous dissiez	vous ayez dit
ils disent	ils dissent	ils aient dit

IMPERATIVE	INFINITIVE	PARTICIPLE
dis	**PRESENT**	**PRESENT**
disons	dire	disant
dites		
	PAST	**PAST**
	avoir dit	dit

VERBS

DORMIR   to sleep

PRESENT	IMPERFECT	FUTURE
je dors	je dormais	je dormirai
tu dors	tu dormais	tu dormiras
il dort	il dormait	il dormira
nous dormons	nous dormions	nous dormirons
vous dormez	vous dormiez	vous dormirez
ils dorment	ils dormaient	ils dormiront

PAST HISTORIC	PERFECT	PLUPERFECT
je dormis	j'ai dormi	j'avais dormi
tu dormis	tu as dormi	tu avais dormi
il dormit	il a dormi	il avait dormi
nous dormîmes	nous avons dormi	nous avions dormi
vous dormîtes	vous avez dormi	vous aviez dormi
ils dormirent	ils ont dormi	ils avaient dormi

CONDITIONAL

PAST ANTERIOR	PRESENT	PAST
j'eus dormi etc	je dormirais	j'aurais dormi
	tu dormirais	tu aurais dormi
	il dormirait	il aurait dormi
	nous dormirions	nous aurions dormi
FUTURE PERFECT	vous dormiriez	vous auriez dormi
j'aurai dormi etc	ils dormiraient	ils auraient dormi

SUBJUNCTIVE

PRESENT	IMPERFECT	PERFECT
je dorme	je dormisse	j'aie dormi
tu dormes	tu dormisses	tu aies dormi
il dorme	il dormît	il ait dormi
nous dormions	nous dormissions	nous ayons dormi
vous dormiez	vous dormissiez	vous ayez dormi
ils dorment	ils dormissent	ils aient dormi

IMPERATIVE	INFINITIVE	PARTICIPLE
dors	PRESENT	PRESENT
dormons	dormir	dormant
dormez		
	PAST	PAST
	avoir dormi	dormi

180

ÉCRIRE   to write

PRESENT	IMPERFECT	FUTURE
j'écris	j'écrivais	j'écrirai
tu écris	tu écrivais	tu écriras
il écrit	il écrivait	il écrira
nous écrivons	nous écrivions	nous écrirons
vous écrivez	vous écriviez	vous écrirez
ils écrivent	ils écrivaient	ils écriront

PAST HISTORIC	PERFECT	PLUPERFECT
j'écrivis	j'ai écrit	j'avais écrit
tu écrivis	tu as écrit	tu avais écrit
il écrivit	il a écrit	il avait écrit
nous écrivîmes	nous avons écrit	nous avions écrit
vous écrivîtes	vous avez écrit	vous aviez écrit
ils écrivirent	ils ont écrit	ils avaient écrit

CONDITIONAL

PAST ANTERIOR	PRESENT	PAST
j'eus écrit etc	j'écrirais	j'aurais écrit
	tu écrirais	tu aurais écrit
	il écrirait	il aurait écrit
	nous écririons	nous aurions écrit
FUTURE PERFECT	vous écririez	vous auriez écrit
j'aurai écrit etc	ils écriraient	ils auraient écrit

SUBJUNCTIVE

PRESENT	IMPERFECT	PERFECT
j'écrive	j'écrivisse	j'aie écrit
tu écrives	tu écrivisses	tu aies écrit
il écrive	il écrivît	il ait écrit
nous écrivions	nous écrivissions	nous ayons écrit
vous écriviez	vous écrivissiez	vous ayez écrit
ils écrivent	ils écrivissent	ils aient écrit

IMPERATIVE	INFINITIVE	PARTICIPLE
écris	**PRESENT**	**PRESENT**
écrivons	écrire	écrivant
écrivez		
	PAST	**PAST**
	avoir écrit	écrit

ESPÉRER   to hope

PRESENT	IMPERFECT	FUTURE
j'espère	j'espérais	j'espérerai
tu espères	tu espérais	tu espéreras
il espère	il espérait	il espérera
nous espérons	nous espérions	nous espérerons
vous espérez	vous espériez	vous espérerez
ils espèrent	ils espéraient	ils espéreront

PAST HISTORIC	PERFECT	PLUPERFECT
j'espérai	j'ai espéré	j'avais espéré
tu espéras	tu as espéré	tu avais espéré
il espéra	il a espéré	il avait espéré
nous espérâmes	nous avons espéré	nous avions espéré
vous espérâtes	vous avez espéré	vous aviez espéré
ils espérèrent	ils ont espéré	ils avaient espéré

CONDITIONAL

PAST ANTERIOR	PRESENT	PAST
j'eus espéré etc	j'espérerais	j'aurais espéré
	tu espérerais	tu aurais espéré
	il espérerait	il aurait espéré
	nous espérerions	nous aurions espéré
FUTURE PERFECT	vous espéreriez	vous auriez espéré
j'aurai espéré etc	ils espéreraient	ils auraient espéré

SUBJUNCTIVE

PRESENT	IMPERFECT	PERFECT
j'espère	j'espérasse	j'aie espéré
tu espères	tu espérasses	tu aies espéré
il espère	il espérât	il ait espéré
nous espérions	nous espérassions	nous ayons espéré
vous espériez	vous espérassiez	vous ayez espéré
ils espèrent	ils espérassent	ils aient espéré

IMPERATIVE	INFINITIVE	PARTICIPLE
espère	**PRESENT**	**PRESENT**
espérons	espérer	espérant
espérez		
	PAST	**PAST**
	avoir espéré	espéré

ÊTRE   to be

PRESENT	IMPERFECT	FUTURE
je suis	j'étais	je serai
tu es	tu étais	tu seras
il est	il était	il sera
nous sommes	nous étions	nous serons
vous êtes	vous étiez	vous serez
ils sont	ils étaient	ils seront

PAST HISTORIC	PERFECT	PLUPERFECT
je fus	j'ai été	j'avais été
tu fus	tu as été	tu avais été
il fut	il a été	il avait été
nous fûmes	nous avons été	nous avions été
vous fûtes	vous avez été	vous aviez été
ils furent	ils ont été	ils avaient été

CONDITIONAL

PAST ANTERIOR	PRESENT	PAST
j'eus été etc	je serais	j'aurais été
	tu serais	tu aurais été
	il serait	il aurait été
	nous serions	nous aurions été
FUTURE PERFECT	vous seriez	vous auriez été
j'aurai été etc	ils seraient	ils auraient été

SUBJUNCTIVE

PRESENT	IMPERFECT	PERFECT
je sois	je fusse	j'aie été
tu sois	tu fusses	tu aies été
il soit	il fût	il ait été
nous soyons	nous fussions	nous ayons été
vous soyez	vous fussiez	vous ayez été
ils soient	ils fussent	ils aient été

IMPERATIVE	INFINITIVE	PARTICIPLE
sois	**PRESENT**	**PRESENT**
soyons	être	étant
soyez		
	PAST	**PAST**
	avoir été	été

VERBS

FAIRE   to do/to make

PRESENT	IMPERFECT	FUTURE
je fais	je faisais	je ferai
tu fais	tu faisais	tu feras
il fait	il faisait	il fera
nous faisons	nous faisions	nous ferons
vous faites	vous faisiez	vous ferez
ils font	ils faisaient	ils feront

PAST HISTORIC	PERFECT	PLUPERFECT
je fis	j'ai fait	j'avais fait
tu fis	tu as fait	tu avais fait
il fit	il a fait	il avait fait
nous fîmes	nous avons fait	nous avions fait
vous fîtes	vous avez fait	vous aviez fait
ils firent	ils ont fait	ils avaient fait

CONDITIONAL

PAST ANTERIOR	PRESENT	PAST
j'eus fait etc	je ferais	j'aurais fait
	tu ferais	tu aurais fait
	il ferait	il aurait fait
	nous ferions	nous aurions fait
FUTURE PERFECT	vous feriez	vous auriez fait
j'aurai fait etc	ils feraient	ils auraient fait

SUBJUNCTIVE

PRESENT	IMPERFECT	PERFECT
je fasse	je fisse	j'aie fait
tu fasses	tu fisses	tu aies fait
il fasse	il fît	il ait fait
nous fassions	nous fissions	nous ayons fait
vous fassiez	vous fissiez	vous ayez fait
ils fassent	ils fissent	ils aient fait

IMPERATIVE	INFINITIVE	PARTICIPLE
fais	**PRESENT**	**PRESENT**
faisons	faire	faisant
faites		
	PAST	**PAST**
	avoir fait	fait

184

FALLOIR   to be necessary

PRESENT	IMPERFECT	FUTURE
il faut	il fallait	il faudra

PAST HISTORIC	PERFECT	PLUPERFECT
il fallut	il a fallu	il avait fallu

CONDITIONAL

PAST ANTERIOR	PRESENT	PAST
il eut fallu	il faudrait	il aurait fallu
FUTURE PERFECT		
il aura fallu		

SUBJUNCTIVE

PRESENT	IMPERFECT	PERFECT
il faille	il fallût	il ait fallu

IMPERATIVE	INFINITIVE	PARTICIPLE
	PRESENT	PRESENT
	falloir	
	PAST	PAST
	avoir fallu	fallu

FINIR   to finish

PRESENT	IMPERFECT	FUTURE
je finis	je finissais	je finirai
tu finis	tu finissais	tu finiras
il finit	il finissait	il finira
nous finissons	nous finissions	nous finirons
vous finissez	vous finissiez	vous finirez
ils finissent	ils finissaient	ils finiront

PAST HISTORIC	PERFECT	PLUPERFECT
je finis	j'ai fini	j'avais fini
tu finis	tu as fini	tu avais fini
il finit	il a fini	il avait fini
nous finîmes	nous avons fini	nous avions fini
vous finîtes	vous avez fini	vous aviez fini
ils finirent	ils ont fini	ils avaient fini

CONDITIONAL

PAST ANTERIOR	PRESENT	PAST
j'eus fini etc	je finirais	j'aurais fini
	tu finirais	tu aurais fini
	il finirait	il aurait fini
	nous finirions	nous aurions fini
FUTURE PERFECT	vous finiriez	vous auriez fini
j'aurai fini etc	ils finiraient	ils auraient fini

SUBJUNCTIVE

PRESENT	IMPERFECT	PERFECT
je finisse	je finisse	j'aie fini
tu finisses	tu finisses	tu aies fini
il finisse	il finît	il ait fini
nous finissions	nous finissions	nous ayons fini
vous finissiez	vous finissiez	vous ayez fini
ils finissent	ils finissent	ils aient fini

IMPERATIVE	INFINITIVE	PARTICIPLE
finis	**PRESENT**	**PRESENT**
finissons	finir	finissant
finissez		
	PAST	**PAST**
	avoir fini	fini

SE MÉFIER to be suspicious

PRESENT
je me méfie
tu te méfies
il se méfie
nous nous méfions
vous vous méfiez
ils se méfient

PAST HISTORIC
je me méfiai
tu te méfias
il se méfia
nous nous méfiâmes
vous vous méfiâtes
ils se méfièrent

IMPERFECT
je me méfiais
tu te méfiais
il se méfiait
nous nous méfiions
vous vous méfiiez
ils se méfiaient

PERFECT
je me suis méfié(e)
tu t'es méfié(e)
il (elle) s'est méfié(e)
nous ns. sommes méfié(e)s
vous vs. êtes méfié(e)(s)
ils (elles) se sont méfié(e)s

FUTURE
je me méfierai
tu te méfieras
il se méfiera
nous nous méfierons
vous vous méfierez
ils se méfieront

PLUPERFECT
je m'étais méfié(e)
tu t'étais méfié(e)
il (elle) s'était méfié(e)
nous ns. étions méfié(e)s
vous vs. étiez méfié(e)(s)
ils (elles) s'étaient méfié(e)s

CONDITIONAL

PAST ANTERIOR
je me fus méfié(e) etc

FUTURE PERFECT
je me serai méfié(e) etc

PRESENT
je me méfierais
tu te méfierais
il se méfierait
nous nous méfierions
vous vous méfieriez
ils se méfieraient

PAST
je me serais méfié(e)
tu te serais méfié(e)
il (elle) se serait méfié(e)
nous ns. serions méfié(e)s
vous vs. seriez méfié(e)(s)
ils (elles) se seraient méfié(e)s

SUBJUNCTIVE

PRESENT
je me méfie
tu te méfies
il se méfie
nous nous méfiions
vous vous méfiiez
ils se méfient

IMPERFECT
je me méfiasse
tu te méfiasses
il se méfiât
nous nous méfiassions
vous vous méfiassiez
ils se méfiassent

PERFECT
je me sois méfié(e)
tu te sois méfié(e)
il (elle) se soit méfié(e)
nous ns. soyons méfié(e)s
vous vs. soyez méfié(e)(s)
ils (elles) se soient méfié(e)s

IMPERATIVE
méfie-toi
méfions-nous
méfiez-vous

INFINITIVE
PRESENT
se méfier

PAST
s'être méfié(e)(s)

PARTICIPLE
PRESENT
se méfiant

PAST
méfié

VERBS

METTRE   to put

PRESENT	IMPERFECT	FUTURE
je mets	je mettais	je mettrai
tu mets	tu mettais	tu mettras
il met	il mettait	il mettra
nous mettons	nous mettions	nous mettrons
vous mettez	vous mettiez	vous mettrez
ils mettent	ils mettaient	ils mettront

PAST HISTORIC	PERFECT	PLUPERFECT
je mis	j'ai mis	j'avais mis
tu mis	tu as mis	tu avais mis
il mit	il a mis	il avait mis
nous mîmes	nous avons mis	nous avions mis
vous mîtes	vous avez mis	vous aviez mis
ils mirent	ils ont mis	ils avaient mis

CONDITIONAL

PAST ANTERIOR	PRESENT	PAST
j'eus mis etc	je mettrais	j'aurais mis
	tu mettrais	tu aurais mis
	il mettrait	il aurait mis
	nous mettrions	nous aurions mis
FUTURE PERFECT	vous mettriez	vous auriez mis
j'aurai mis etc	ils mettraient	ils auraient mis

SUBJUNCTIVE

PRESENT	IMPERFECT	PERFECT
je mette	je misse	j'aie mis
tu mettes	tu misses	tu aies mis
il mette	il mît	il ait mis
nous mettions	nous missions	nous ayons mis
vous mettiez	vous missiez	vous ayez mis
ils mettent	ils missent	ils aient mis

IMPERATIVE	INFINITIVE	PARTICIPLE
mets	PRESENT	PRESENT
mettons	mettre	mettant
mettez		
	PAST	PAST
	avoir mis	mis

OUVRIR   to open

PRESENT	IMPERFECT	FUTURE
j'ouvre	j'ouvrais	j'ouvrirai
tu ouvres	tu ouvrais	tu ouvriras
il ouvre	il ouvrait	il ouvrira
nous ouvrons	nous ouvrions	nous ouvrirons
vous ouvrez	vous ouvriez	vous ouvrirez
ils ouvrent	ils ouvraient	ils ouvriront

PAST HISTORIC	PERFECT	PLUPERFECT
j'ouvris	j'ai ouvert	j'avais ouvert
tu ouvris	tu as ouvert	tu avais ouvert
il ouvrit	il a ouvert	il avait ouvert
nous ouvrîmes	nous avons ouvert	nous avions ouvert
vous ouvrîtes	vous avez ouvert	vous aviez ouvert
ils ouvrirent	ils ont ouvert	ils avaient ouvert

CONDITIONAL

PAST ANTERIOR	PRESENT	PAST
j'eus ouvert etc	j'ouvrirais	j'aurais ouvert
	tu ouvrirais	tu aurais ouvert
	il ouvrirait	il aurait ouvert
	nous ouvririons	nous aurions ouvert
FUTURE PERFECT	vous ouvririez	vous auriez ouvert
j'aurai ouvert etc	ils ouvriraient	ils auraient ouvert

SUBJUNCTIVE

PRESENT	IMPERFECT	PERFECT
j'ouvre	j'ouvrisse	j'aie ouvert
tu ouvres	tu ouvrisses	tu aies ouvert
il ouvre	il ouvrît	il ait ouvert
nous ouvrions	nous ouvrissions	nous ayons ouvert
vous ouvriez	vous ouvrissiez	vous ayez ouvert
ils ouvrent	ils ouvrissent	ils aient ouvert

IMPERATIVE	INFINITIVE	PARTICIPLE
ouvre	PRESENT	PRESENT
ouvrons	ouvrir	ouvrant
ouvrez		
	PAST	PAST
	avoir ouvert	ouvert

POUVOIR   to be able to

PRESENT	IMPERFECT	FUTURE
je peux	je pouvais	je pourrai
tu peux	tu pouvais	tu pourras
il peut	il pouvait	il pourra
nous pouvons	nous pouvions	nous pourrons
vous pouvez	vous pouviez	vous pourrez
ils peuvent	ils pouvaient	ils pourront

PAST HISTORIC	PERFECT	PLUPERFECT
je pus	j'ai pu	j'avais pu
tu pus	tu as pu	tu avais pu
il put	il a pu	il avait pu
nous pûmes	nous avons pu	nous avions pu
vous pûtes	vous avez pu	vous aviez pu
ils purent	ils ont pu	ils avaient pu

CONDITIONAL

PAST ANTERIOR	PRESENT	PAST
j'eus pu etc	je pourrais	j'aurais pu
	tu pourrais	tu aurais pu
	il pourrait	il aurait pu
	nous pourrions	nous aurions pu
FUTURE PERFECT	vous pourriez	vous auriez pu
j'aurai pu etc	ils pourraient	ils auraient pu

SUBJUNCTIVE

PRESENT	IMPERFECT	PERFECT
je puisse	je pusse	j'aie pu
tu puisses	tu pusses	tu aies pu
il puisse	il pût	il ait pu
nous puissions	nous pussions	nous ayons pu
vous puissiez	vous pussiez	vous ayez pu
ils puissent	ils pussent	ils aient pu

IMPERATIVE	INFINITIVE	PARTICIPLE
	PRESENT	**PRESENT**
	pouvoir	pouvant
	PAST	**PAST**
	avoir pu	pu

PRENDRE   to take

PRESENT	IMPERFECT	FUTURE
je prends	je prenais	je prendrai
tu prends	tu prenais	tu prendras
il prend	il prenait	il prendra
nous prenons	nous prenions	nous prendrons
vous prenez	vous preniez	vous prendrez
ils prennent	ils prenaient	ils prendront

PAST HISTORIC	PERFECT	PLUPERFECT
je pris	j'ai pris	j'avais pris
tu pris	tu as pris	tu avais pris
il prit	il a pris	il avait pris
nous prîmes	nous avons pris	nous avions pris
vous prîtes	vous avez pris	vous aviez pris
ils prirent	ils ont pris	ils avaient pris

CONDITIONAL

PAST ANTERIOR	PRESENT	PAST
j'eus pris etc	je prendrais	j'aurais pris
	tu prendrais	tu aurais pris
	il prendrait	il aurait pris
	nous prendrions	nous aurions pris
FUTURE PERFECT	vous prendriez	vous auriez pris
j'aurai pris etc	ils prendraient	ils auraient pris

SUBJUNCTIVE

PRESENT	IMPERFECT	PERFECT
je prenne	je prisse	j'aie pris
tu prennes	tu prisses	tu aies pris
il prenne	il prît	il ait pris
nous prenions	nous prissions	nous ayons pris
vous preniez	vous prissiez	vous ayez pris
ils prennent	ils prissent	ils aient pris

IMPERATIVE	INFINITIVE	PARTICIPLE
	PRESENT	PRESENT
prends	prendre	prenant
prenons		
prenez		
	PAST	PAST
	avoir pris	pris

VERBS

RECEVOIR · to receive

PRESENT	IMPERFECT	FUTURE
je reçois	je recevais	je recevrai
tu reçois	tu recevais	tu recevras
il reçoit	il recevait	il recevra
nous recevons	nous recevions	nous recevrons
vous recevez	vous receviez	vous recevrez
ils reçoivent	ils recevaient	ils recevront

PAST HISTORIC	PERFECT	PLUPERFECT
je reçus	j'ai reçu	j'avais reçu
tu reçus	tu as reçu	tu avais reçu
il reçut	il a reçu	il avait reçu
nous reçûmes	nous avons reçu	nous avions reçu
vous reçûtes	vous avez reçu	vous aviez reçu
ils reçurent	ils ont reçu	ils avaient reçu

CONDITIONAL

PAST ANTERIOR	PRESENT	PAST
j'eus reçu etc.	je recevrais	j'aurais reçu
	tu recevrais	tu aurais reçu
	il recevrait	il aurait reçu
	nous recevrions	nous aurions reçu
FUTURE PERFECT	vous recevriez	vous auriez reçu
j'aurai reçu etc	ils recevraient	ils auraient reçu

SUBJUNCTIVE

PRESENT	IMPERFECT	PERFECT
je reçoive	je reçusse	j'aie reçu
tu reçoives	tu reçusses	tu aies reçu
il reçoive	il reçût	il ait reçu
nous recevions	nous reçussions	nous ayons reçu
vous receviez	vous reçussiez	vous ayez reçu
ils reçoivent	ils reçussent	ils aient reçu

IMPERATIVE	INFINITIVE	PARTICIPLE
reçois	PRESENT	PRESENT
recevons	recevoir	recevant
recevez		
	PAST	PAST
	avoir reçu	reçu

SAVOIR   to know

PRESENT	IMPERFECT	FUTURE
je sais	je savais	je saurai
tu sais	tu savais	tu sauras
il sait	il savait	il saura
nous savons	nous savions	nous saurons
vous savez	vous saviez	vous saurez
ils savent	ils savaient	ils sauront

PAST HISTORIC	PERFECT	PLUPERFECT
je sus	j'ai su	j'avais su
tu sus	tu as su	tu avais su
il sut	il a su	il avait su
nous sûmes	nous avons su	nous avions su
vous sûtes	vous avez su	vous aviez su
ils surent	ils ont su	ils avaient su

CONDITIONAL

PAST ANTERIOR	PRESENT	PAST
j'eus su etc	je saurais	j'aurais su
	tu saurais	tu aurais su
	il saurait	il aurait su
	nous saurions	nous aurions su
FUTURE PERFECT	vous sauriez	vous auriez su
j'aurai su etc	ils sauraient	ils auraient su

SUBJUNCTIVE

PRESENT	IMPERFECT	PERFECT
je sache	je susse	j'aie su
tu saches	tu susses	tu aies su
il sache	il sût	il ait su
nous sachions	nous sussions	nous ayons su
vous sachiez	vous sussiez	vous ayez su
ils sachent	ils sussent	ils aient su

IMPERATIVE	INFINITIVE	PARTICIPLE
sache	PRESENT	PRESENT
sachons	savoir	sachant
sachez		
	PAST	PAST
	avoir su	su

TENIR   to hold

PRESENT	IMPERFECT	FUTURE
je tiens	je tenais	je tiendrai
tu tiens	tu tenais	tu tiendras
il tient	il tenait	il tiendra
nous tenons	nous tenions	nous tiendrons
vous tenez	vous teniez	vous tiendrez
ils tiennent	ils tenaient	ils tiendront

PAST HISTORIC	PERFECT	PLUPERFECT
je tins	j'ai tenu	j'avais tenu
tu tins	tu as tenu	tu avais tenu
il tint	il a tenu	il avait tenu
nous tînmes	nous avons tenu	nous avions tenu
vous tîntes	vous avez tenu	vous aviez tenu
ils tinrent	ils ont tenu	ils avaient tenu

CONDITIONAL

PAST ANTERIOR	PRESENT	PAST
j'eus tenu etc	je tiendrais	j'aurais tenu
	tu tiendrais	tu aurais tenu
	il tiendrait	il aurait tenu
	nous tiendrions	nous aurions tenu
FUTURE PERFECT	vous tiendriez	vous auriez tenu
j'aurai tenu etc	ils tiendraient	ils auraient tenu

SUBJUNCTIVE

PRESENT	IMPERFECT	PERFECT
je tienne	je tinsse	j'aie tenu
tu tiennes	tu tinsses	tu aies tenu
il tienne	il tînt	il ait tenu
nous tenions	nous tinssions	nous ayons tenu
vous teniez	vous tinssiez	vous ayez tenu
ils tiennent	ils tinssent	ils aient tenu

IMPERATIVE	INFINITIVE	PARTICIPLE
tiens	**PRESENT**	**PRESENT**
tenons	tenir	tenant
tenez		
	PAST	**PAST**
	avoir tenu	tenu

VENDRE   to sell

PRESENT	IMPERFECT	FUTURE
je vends	je vendais	je vendrai
tu vends	tu vendais	tu vendras
il vend	il vendait	il vendra
nous vendons	nous vendions	nous vendrons
vous vendez	vous vendiez	vous vendrez
ils vendent	ils vendaient	ils vendront

PAST HISTORIC	PERFECT	PLUPERFECT
je vendis	j'ai vendu	j'avais vendu
tu vendis	tu as vendu	tu avais vendu
il vendit	il a vendu	il avait vendu
nous vendîmes	nous avons vendu	nous avions vendu
vous vendîtes	vous avez vendu	vous aviez vendu
ils vendirent	ils ont vendu	ils avaient vendu

CONDITIONAL

PAST ANTERIOR	PRESENT	PAST
j'eus vendu etc	je vendrais	j'aurais vendu
	tu vendrais	tu aurais vendu
	il vendrait	il aurait vendu
	nous vendrions	nous aurions vendu
FUTURE PERFECT	vous vendriez	vous auriez vendu
j'aurai vendu etc	ils vendraient	ils auraient vendu

SUBJUNCTIVE

PRESENT	IMPERFECT	PERFECT
je vende	je vendisse	j'aie vendu
tu vendes	tu vendisses	tu aies vendu
il vende	il vendît	il ait vendu
nous vendions	nous vendissions	nous ayons vendu
vous vendiez	vous vendissiez	vous ayez vendu
ils vendent	ils vendissent	ils aient vendu

IMPERATIVE	INFINITIVE	PARTICIPLE
vends	**PRESENT**	**PRESENT**
vendons	vendre	vendant
vendez		
	PAST	**PAST**
	avoir vendu	vendu

VENIR   to come

PRESENT	IMPERFECT	FUTURE
je viens	je venais	je viendrai
tu viens	tu venais	tu viendras
il vient	il venait	il viendra
nous venons	nous venions	nous viendrons
vous venez	vous veniez	vous viendrez
ils viennent	ils venaient	ils viendront

PAST HISTORIC	PERFECT	PLUPERFECT
je vins	je suis venu(e)	j'étais venu(e)
tu vins	tu es venu(e)	tu étais venu(e)
il vint	il (elle) est venu(e)	il (elle) était venu(e)
nous vînmes	nous sommes venu(e)s	nous étions venu(e)s
vous vîntes	vous êtes venu(e)(s)	vous étiez venu(e)(s)
ils vinrent	ils (elles) sont venu(e)s	ils (elles) étaient venu(e)s

CONDITIONAL

PAST ANTERIOR	PRESENT	PAST
je fus venu(e) etc	je viendrais	je serais venu(e)
	tu viendrais	tu serais venu(e)
	il viendrait	il (elle) serait venu(e)
	nous viendrions	nous serions venu(e)s
FUTURE PERFECT	vous viendriez	vous seriez venu(e)(s)
je serai venu(e) etc	ils viendraient	ils (elles) seraient venu(e)s

SUBJUNCTIVE

PRESENT	IMPERFECT	PERFECT
je vienne	je vinsse	je sois venu(e)
tu viennes	tu vinsses	tu sois venu(e)
il vienne	il vînt	il (elle) soit venu(e)
nous venions	nous vinssions	nous soyons venu(e)s
vous veniez	vous vinssiez	vous soyez venu(e)(s)
ils viennent	ils vinssent	ils (elles) soient venu(e)s

IMPERATIVE	INFINITIVE	PARTICIPLE
viens	**PRESENT**	**PRESENT**
venons	venir	venant
venez		
	PAST	**PAST**
	être venu(e)(s)	venu

VIVRE to live

PRESENT	IMPERFECT	FUTURE
je vis	je vivais	je vivrai
tu vis	tu vivais	tu vivras
il vit	il vivait	il vivra
nous vivons	nous vivions	nous vivrons
vous vivez	vous viviez	vous vivrez
ils vivent	ils vivaient	ils vivront

PAST HISTORIC	PERFECT	PLUPERFECT
je vécus	j'ai vécu	j'avais vécu
tu vécus	tu as vécu	tu avais vécu
il vécut	il a vécu	il avait vécu
nous vécûmes	nous avons vécu	nous avions vécu
vous vécûtes	vous avez vécu	vous aviez vécu
ils vécurent	ils ont vécu	ils avaient vécu

CONDITIONAL

PAST ANTERIOR	PRESENT	PAST
j'eus vécu etc	je vivrais	j'aurais vécu
	tu vivrais	tu aurais vécu
	il vivrait	il aurait vécu
	nous vivrions	nous aurions vécu
FUTURE PERFECT	vous vivriez	vous auriez vécu
j'aurai vécu etc	ils vivraient	ils auraient vécu

SUBJUNCTIVE

PRESENT	IMPERFECT	PERFECT
je vive	je vécusse	j'aie vécu
tu vives	tu vécusses	tu aies vécu
il vive	il vécût	il ait vécu
nous vivions	nous vécussions	nous ayons vécu
vous viviez	vous vécussiez	vous ayez vécu
ils vivent	ils vécussent	ils aient vécu

IMPERATIVE	INFINITIVE	PARTICIPLE
vis	PRESENT	PRESENT
vivons	vivre	vivant
vivez		
	PAST	PAST
	avoir vécu	vécu

VOIR

to see

PRESENT	IMPERFECT	FUTURE
je vois	je voyais	je verrai
tu vois	tu voyais	tu verras
il voit	il voyait	il verra
nous voyons	nous voyions	nous verrons
vous voyez	vous voyiez	vous verrez
ils voient	ils voyaient	ils verront

PAST HISTORIC	PERFECT	PLUPERFECT
je vis	j'ai vu	j'avais vu
tu vis	tu as vu	tu avais vu
il vit	il a vu	il avait vu
nous vîmes	nous avons vu	nous avions vu
vous vîtes	vous avez vu	vous aviez vu
ils virent	ils ont vu	ils avaient vu

CONDITIONAL

PAST ANTERIOR	PRESENT	PAST
j'eus vu etc	je verrais	j'aurais vu
	tu verrais	tu aurais vu
	il verrait	il aurait vu
	nous verrions	nous aurions vu
FUTURE PERFECT	vous verriez	vous auriez vu
j'aurai vu etc	ils verraient	ils auraient vu

SUBJUNCTIVE

PRESENT	IMPERFECT	PERFECT
je voie	je visse	j'aie vu
tu voies	tu visses	tu aies vu
il voie	il vît	il ait vu
nous voyions	nous vissions	nous ayons vu
vous voyiez	vous vissiez	vous ayez vu
ils voient	ils vissent	ils aient vu

IMPERATIVE	INFINITIVE	PARTICIPLE
vois	PRESENT	PRESENT
voyons	voir	voyant
voyez		
	PAST	PAST
	avoir vu	vu

VOULOIR   to want

PRESENT	IMPERFECT	FUTURE
je veux	je voulais	je voudrai
tu veux	tu voulais	tu voudras
il veut	il voulait	il voudra
nous voulons	nous voulions	nous voudrons
vous voulez	vous vouliez	vous voudrez
ils veulent	ils voulaient	ils voudront

PAST HISTORIC	PERFECT	PLUPERFECT
je voulus	j'ai voulu	j'avais voulu
tu voulus	tu as voulu	tu avais voulu
il voulut	il a voulu	il avait voulu
nous voulûmes	nous avons voulu	nous avions voulu
vous voulûtes	vous avez voulu	vous aviez voulu
ils voulurent	ils ont voulu	ils avaient voulu

CONDITIONAL

PAST ANTERIOR	PRESENT	PAST
j'eus voulu etc	je voudrais	j'aurais voulu
	tu voudrais	tu aurais voulu
	il voudrait	il aurait voulu
	nous voudrions	nous aurions voulu
FUTURE PERFECT	vous voudriez	vous auriez voulu
j'aurai voulu etc	ils voudraient	ils auraient voulu

SUBJUNCTIVE

PRESENT	IMPERFECT	PERFECT
je veuille	je voulusse	j'aie voulu
tu veuilles	tu voulusses	tu aies voulu
il veuille	il voulût	il ait voulu
nous voulions	nous voulussions	nous ayons voulu
vous vouliez	vous voulussiez	vous ayez voulu
ils veuillent	ils voulussent	ils aient voulu

IMPERATIVE	INFINITIVE	PARTICIPLE
veuille	**PRESENT**	**PRESENT**
veuillons	vouloir	voulant
veuillez		
	PAST	**PAST**
	avoir voulu	voulu

M. Verbal Constructions

There are two main types of verbal construction:

1. Verbs followed by an infinitive

There are three main types of construction when a verb is followed by an infinitive. For examples of all three types, see pp 146-54.

a) *Verbs followed by an infinitive without any linking preposition*

These include verbs of wishing and willing, of movement and of perception:

adorer to love	**aimer** to like	**aimer mieux** to prefer
aller to go (and)	**compter** to intend to	**descendre** to go down (and)
désirer to wish	**détester** to hate	**devoir** to have to
écouter to listen to	**entendre** to hear	**entrer** to go in (and)
envoyer to send	**espérer** to hope to	**faire** to make
falloir to have to	**laisser** to let	**monter** to go up (and)
oser to dare	**pouvoir** to be able to	**préférer** to prefer to
regarder to watch	**rentrer** to go in/back (and)	**savoir** to know how to
sembler to seem to	**sentir** to feel	**sortir** to go out (and)
souhaiter to wish to	**valoir mieux** to be better to	**venir** to come (and)
voir to see	**vouloir** to want to	

b) *Verbs followed by à + infinitive*

aider à	to help (to do)
s'amuser à	to enjoy (doing)
apprendre à	to learn (to do)
s'apprêter à	to get ready (to do)
arriver à	to manage (to do)
s'attendre à	to expect (to do)
autoriser à	to allow (to do)
chercher à	to try (to do)
commencer à	to start (doing)
consentir à	to agree (to do)
consister à	to consist in (doing)
continuer à	to continue (to do)
se décider à	to make up one's mind (to do)
encourager à	to encourage (to do)
enseigner à	to teach how (to do)
forcer à	to force (to do)
s'habituer à	to get used (to doing)
hésiter à	to hesitate (to do)
inciter à	to prompt (to do)
s'intéresser à	to be interested in (doing)
inviter à	to invite (to do)
se mettre à	to start (doing)
obliger à	to force (to do)
parvenir à	to succeed (in doing)
passer son temps à	to spend one's time (doing)
perdre son temps à	to waste one's time (doing)
persister à	to persist in (doing)
pousser à	to urge (to do)
se préparer à	to get ready (to do)
renoncer à	to give up (doing)
rester à	to be left (to do)
réussir à	to manage (to do)
servir à	to be used for (doing)
songer à	to think of (doing)
tarder à	to delay/be late in (doing)
tenir à	to be keen (to do)

c) *Verbs followed by* ***de*** + infinitive:

accepter de	to agree (to do)
accuser de	to accuse of (doing)
achever de	to finish (doing)
s'arrêter de	to stop (doing)
avoir besoin de	to need (to do)
avoir envie de	to feel like (doing)
avoir peur de	to be afraid (to do)
cesser de	to stop (doing)
se charger de	to undertake (to do)
commander de	to order (to do)
conseiller de	to advise (to do)
se contenter de	to make do with (doing)
craindre de	to be afraid (to do)
décider de	to decide (to do)
déconseiller de	to advise against (doing)
défendre de	to forbid (to do)
demander de	to ask (to do)
se dépêcher de	to hasten (to do)
dire de	to tell (to do)
dissuader de	to dissuade from (doing)
s'efforcer de	to strive (to do)
empêcher de	to prevent (from doing)
s'empresser de	to hasten (to do)
entreprendre de	to undertake (to do)
essayer de	to try (to do)
s'étonner de	to be surprised (at doing)
éviter de	to avoid (doing)
s'excuser de	to apologize for (doing)
faire semblant de	to pretend (to do)
feindre de	to pretend (to do)
finir de	to finish (doing)
se garder de	to be careful not to (do)
se hâter de	to hasten (to do)
interdire de	to forbid (to do)
jurer de	to swear (to do)
manquer de	'to nearly' (do)
menacer de	to threaten (to do)
mériter de	to deserve (to do)
négliger de	to fail (to do)

s'occuper de	to undertake (to do)
offrir de	to offer (to do)
omettre de	to omit (to do)
ordonner de	to order (to do)
oublier de	to forget (to do)
permettre de	to allow (to do)
persuader de	to persuade (to do)
prier de	to ask (to do)
promettre de	to promise (to do)
proposer de	to offer (to do)
recommander de	to recommend (to do)
refuser de	to refuse (to do)
regretter de	to be sorry (to do)
remercier de	to thank for (doing)
résoudre de	to resolve (to do)
risquer de	to risk (doing)
se souvenir de	to remember (doing)
suggérer de	to suggest (doing)
supplier de	to implore (to do)
tâcher de	to try (to do)
tenter de	to try (to do)
venir de	to have just (done)

2. Verbs followed by an object

In general, verbs which take a direct object in French also take a direct object in English, and verbs which take an indirect object in French (ie verb + preposition + object) also take an indirect object in English. There are, however, some exceptions:

a) *Verbs followed by an indirect object in English but not in French* (the English preposition is not translated):

attendre	to wait for
chercher	to look for
demander	to ask for
écouter	to listen to
espérer	to hope for
payer	to pay for
regarder	to look at
reprocher	to blame for

on a demandé l'addition we asked for the bill	**j'attendais l'autobus** I was waiting for the bus
je cherche mon frère I'm looking for my brother	**tu écoutes la radio?** are you listening to the radio?

b) *Verbs which take a direct object in English, but an indirect object in French:*

convenir à	to suit
se fier à	to trust
jouer à	to play *(game, sport)*
jouer de	to play *(musical instrument)*
obéir à	to obey
désobéir à	to disobey
pardonner à	to forgive
renoncer à	to give up
répondre à	to answer
résister à	to resist
ressembler à	to resemble (to look like)
téléphoner à	to phone

tu peux te fier à moi you can trust me	**tu joues souvent au tennis?** do you often play tennis?
il joue bien de la guitare he plays the guitar well	**tu as répondu à ma lettre?** did you answer my letter?
téléphonons au médecin let's phone the doctor	**obéis à ton père!** obey your father!

c) *Verbs which take a direct object in English but **de** + indirect object in French:*

s'apercevoir de	to notice
s'approcher de	to come near
avoir besoin de	to need
changer de	to change
douter de	to doubt
se douter de	to suspect
s'emparer de	to seize, to grab
jouir de	to enjoy
manquer de	to lack, to miss
se méfier de	to mistrust
se servir de	to use
se souvenir de	to remember
se tromper de …	to get the wrong …

je dois changer de train?
do I have to change trains?

il ne s'est aperçu de rien
he didn't notice anything

méfiez-vous de lui
don't trust him

je me servirai de ton vélo
I'll use your bike

tu te souviens de Jean?
do you remember Jean?

il s'est trompé de numéro
he got the wrong number

d) *Some verbs take à or de before an object, whereas their English equivalent uses a different preposition:*

i) Verb + **à** + object:

croire à   to believe in
s'intéresser à   to be interested in
penser à   to think of/about
songer à   to think of
rêver à   to dream of/about
servir à   to be used for

je m'intéresse au football et à la course automobile
I'm interested in football and in motor-racing

à quoi penses-tu?   ça sert à quoi?
what are you thinking about? what is this used for?

ii) Verb + **de** + object:

dépendre de   to depend on
être fâché de   to be annoyed at
féliciter de   to congratulate for
parler de   to speak of/about
remercier de   to thank for
rire de   to laugh at
traiter de   to deal with, to be about
vivre de   to live on

cela dépendra du temps   il m'a parlé de toi
it'll depend on the weather he told me about you

tu l'as remercié du cadeau qu'il t'a fait?
did you thank him for the present he gave you?

3. Verbs followed by one direct object and one indirect object

a) In general, these are verbs of giving or lending, and their English equivalents are constructed in the same way, eg:

> **donner quelque chose à quelqu'un**
> to give something to someone

> **il a vendu son ordinateur à son voisin**
> he sold his computer to his neighbour

Note that after such verbs, the preposition 'to' is often omitted in English but **à**, however, cannot be omitted in French. Particular care must be taken when object pronouns are used with these verbs (see pp 80-1).

b) With verbs expressing 'taking away', **à** is translated by 'from' (**qn** stands for 'quelqu'un' and **sb** for 'somebody'):

acheter à qn	to buy from sb
cacher à qn	to hide from sb
demander à qn	to ask sb for
emprunter à qn	to borrow from sb
enlever à qn	to take away from sb
ôter à qn	to take away from sb
prendre à qn	to take from sb
voler à qn	to steal from sb

> **à qui as-tu emprunté cela?**   **il l'a volé à son frère**
> who did you borrow this from?   he stole it from his brother

4. Verb + indirect object + 'de' + infinitive

Some verbs which take a direct object in English are followed by **à** + object + **de** + infinitive in French:

commander à qn de faire	to order sb to do
conseiller à qn de faire	to advise sb to do
défendre à qn de faire	to forbid sb to do
demander à qn de faire	to ask sb to do
dire à qn de faire	to tell sb to do
ordonner à qn de faire	to order sb to do
permettre à qn de faire	to allow sb to do
promettre à qn de faire	to promise sb to do
proposer à qn de faire	to offer to do for sb, to suggest to sb to do

je leur ai conseillé de ne pas essayer
I advised them not to try

demande à ton fils de t'aider
ask your son to help you

j'ai promis à mes parents de ne jamais recommencer
I promised my parents never to do this again

8. PREPOSITIONS

Prepositions in both French and English can have many different meanings, which presents considerable difficulties for the translator. The following guide to the most common prepositions sets out the generally accepted meanings on the left, with a description of their use in brackets, and an illustration. The main meanings are given first. Prepositions are listed in alphabetical order.

• à •

at	(place)	**au troisième arrêt** at the third stop
	(date)	**à Noël** at Christmas
	(time)	**à trois heures** at three o'clock
	(idiom)	**au hasard** at random **au travail** at work
in	(place)	**à Montmartre** in Montmartre **à Lyon** in Lyons **au supermarché** in the supermarket **à la campagne** in the country **au lit** in bed **au loin** in the distance
	(manner)	**à la française** in the French way

		à ma façon my way
to	(place)	**aller au théâtre** to go to the theatre **aller à Londres** to go to London
	(+ infinitive)	**c'est facile à faire** it is easy to do *(see pp 150-1)*
away from	(distance)	**à 3 km d'ici** 3 km away
by	(means)	**aller à vélo** to go by bike **je l'ai reconnu à ses habits** I recognized him by his clothing
	(manner)	**fait à la main** hand-made
	(rate)	**à la centaine** by the hundred **100 km à l'heure** 100 km per hour
for/up to	(+ pronoun)	**c'est à vous de jouer** it's your turn **c'est à nous de te le dire** it's up to us to tell you
	(purpose)	**une tasse à café** a coffee cup
from		**il l'a caché à ses parents** he hid it from his parents
his/her/my etc	(possessive)	**son sac à elle** her bag
on	(means)	**aller à cheval/à pied** to go on horseback/on foot

PREPOSITIONS

	(place)	**à la page 12** on page 12 **à droite/à gauche** on/to the right/left
	(time)	**à cette occasion** on this occasion
with	(descriptive)	**un homme aux cheveux blonds** a man with blond hair **l'homme à la valise** the man with the case
	(idiom)	**à bras ouverts** with open arms

For use of the preposition à with the infinitive see verbal constructions p 201.

• après •

after	(time)	**après votre arrivée** after your arrival
	(sequence)	**24 ans après la mort du président** 24 years after the death of the President **je suis allé au lit après avoir fini le livre** I went to bed after I finished the book **après s'être séparée de son mari** after separating from her husband

• auprès de •

beside	**il s'assit auprès de sa mère** he sat down beside his mother
compared to	**ce n'est rien auprès de ce que tu as fait** it's nothing compared to what you've done

.avant.

before	(time)	**avant cet après-midi** before this afternoon **avant ce soir** before tonight **avant de s'asseoir** before sitting down
	(preference)	**la famille avant tout** the family comes first (above all else)

.avec.

with	(association)	**je viendrai avec lui** I'll come with him
	(means)	**elle marche avec une canne** she walks with a stick

.chez.

at	(place)	**chez moi/toi** at/to my/your house **chez mon oncle** at my uncle's **chez le pharmacien** at the chemist's
among		**chez les Écossais** among the Scots
about		**ce qui m'énerve chez toi, c'est …** what annoys me about you is …
in		**chez Sartre** in Sartre's work

.contre.

against	(place)	**contre le mur** against the wall

with	(after verb)	**je suis fâché contre elle** I'm angry with her
for		**elle a échangé un billet contre des pièces** she changed a note for coins

.dans.

in	(position)	**dans ma serviette** in my briefcase
	(time)	**je pars dans deux jours** I'm leaving in two days' time
	(idiom)	**dans l'attente de vous voir** looking forward to seeing you
from	(removal)	**prendre quelque chose dans l'armoire** to take something from the cupboard
on	(position)	**dans le train** on the train
out of	(idiom)	**boire dans un verre** to drink out of a glass

.de.

from	(place)	**je suis venu de Glasgow** I have come from Glasgow
	(date)	**du 5 février au 10 mars** from 5 February to 10 March **d'un week-end à l'autre** from one weekend to another
of	(adjectival)	**un cri de triomphe** a shout of triumph
	(contents)	**une tasse de café** a cup of coffee

	(cause)	**mourir de faim** to die of hunger
	(measurement)	**long de 3 mètres** 3 metres long
	(time)	**ma montre retarde de 10 minutes** my watch is 10 minutes slow
	(price)	**le montant est de 20 euros** the total is 20 euros
	(possessive)	**la père de mon ami** my friend's father
	(adjectival)	**les vacances de Pâques** the Easter holidays
	(after 'quelque chose')	**quelque chose de bon** something good
	(after 'rien')	**rien de nouveau** nothing new
	(after 'personne')	**personne d'autre** nobody else
	(quantity)	**beaucoup de, peu de** many, few
by	(idiom)	**je le connais de vue** I know him by sight
in	(manner)	**de cette façon** in this way
	(after superlatives)	**la plus haute montagne d'Écosse** the highest mountain in Scotland
on	(position)	**de ce côté** on this side
than	(comparative)	**moins de 2 euros** less than 2 euros **plus de 3 litres** more than 3 litres

to	(after adjectives)	**ravi de vous voir** delighted to see you **il est facile de se tromper** it is easy to make a mistake
	(after verbs)	**s'efforcer de** to try to
with	(cause)	**tomber de fatigue** to drop with exhaustion

.depuis.

for	(time)	**j'étudie le français depuis 3 ans** I have been studying French for 3 years **j'étudiais le français depuis 3 ans** I had been studying French for 3 years **je n'y ai pas joué depuis des années** I haven't played for years
from	(place)	**depuis ma fenêtre, je vois la mer** from my window I can see the sea
	(time)	**depuis le matin jusqu'au soir** from morning till evening
since		**depuis dimanche** since Sunday

.derrière.

behind	(place)	**derrière la maison** behind the house

.dès.

from	(time)	**dès six heures** from six o'clock onwards **dès 1934** as far back as 1934 **dès le début** from the beginning

		dès maintenant from now on
	(place)	**dès Édimbourg** from (the moment of leaving) Edinburgh

.devant.

in front of	(place)	**devant l'école** in front of the school
before	(place)	**sur la table devant eux** on the table before them

.en.

in	(place)	**être en ville** to be in town **en Angleterre** in England
	(colour)	**un mur peint en jaune** a wall painted yellow
	(material)	**une montre en or** a gold watch
by	(means)	**en auto/en avion** by car/by plane
	(dates, seasons)	**en quelle année?** in what year? **en 2002** in 2002 **en été** in the summer **en juillet** in July
	(dress)	**en jupe** in a skirt
	(language)	**en chinois** in Chinese

	(time)	**j'ai fait mes devoirs en 20 minutes** I did my homework in 20 minutes
like, as		**il s'est habillé en femme** he dressed as a woman
on	(idiom)	**en vacances** on holiday **en moyenne** on average
	(+ present participle)	**en faisant** on/while/by doing

*Note that **en** is not used with the definite article except in certain expressions:*
***en l'an 2020** (in the year 2020),* **en l'honneur de** *(in honour of) and* **en la présence de** *(in the presence of).*

.en tant que.

| *as/in one's capacity as* | **en tant que professeur**
as a teacher |

.entre.

among		**être entre amis** to be among friends
between	(place)	**entre Londres et Paris** between London and Paris
	(time)	**entre 6 et 10 heures** between 6 and 10 o'clock
	(idiom)	**entre nous** between you and me
in	(punctuation)	**entre guillemets** in inverted commas **entre parenthèses** in brackets

.d'entre.

| *of/from among* | **certains d'entre eux**
some of them |

.envers.

to/towards	**être bien disposé envers quelqu'un** to be well-disposed towards someone

.hors de.

out of	**hors de danger** out of danger

.jusque.

up to/as far as	(place)	**jusqu'à la frontière espagnole** as far as the Spanish border
	(time)	**jusqu'ici** up to now **jusque-là** up till then
till		**jusqu'à demain** till tomorrow

.malgré.

in spite of	**malgré la chaleur** in spite of the heat

.par.

by	(agent)	**la décision fut prise par le président** the decision was made by the President
	(means of transport)	**par le train** by train
	(distributive)	**trois fois par semaine** three times a week **deux par deux** two by two
	(place)	**par ici/là** this/that way

in/on	(weather)	**par un temps pareil** in such weather
		par un beau jour d'hiver on a beautiful winter's day
through/out of	(place)	**regarder par la fenêtre** to look out of the window
		jette-le par la fenêtre throw it out of the window
to/on		**tomber par terre** to fall to the ground
		étendu par terre lying on the ground
	(+ infinitive)	**commencer/finir par faire** to begin/end by doing

.parmi.

| *among* | | **parmi mes ennemis**
among my enemies |

.pendant.

| *for* | (time) | **il l'avait fait pendant 5 ans**
he had done it for 5 years |
| *during* | | **pendant l'été**
during the summer |

.pour.

for		**ce livre est pour vous** this book is for you
		mourir pour la patrie to die for one's country
	(purpose)	**c'est pour cela que je suis venu** that's why I've come
	(emphatic)	**pour moi, cet argument ne tient pas** if you ask me, this argument isn't valid

	(time)	**j'en ai pour une heure**
		it'll take me an hour
		je suis en vacances pour 2 semaines
		I'm on holiday for 2 weeks

*(**pour** stresses intention and future time: see **depuis** and **pendant**, pp 214 and 218)*

	(idiom)	**c'est bon pour la santé**
		it's good for your health
to	(+ infinitive)	**il était trop paresseux pour réussir ses examens**
		he was too lazy to pass his exams

.près de.

near	(place)	**près du marché**
		near the market
nearly	(time)	**il est près de minuit**
		it's nearly midnight
	(quantity)	**près de cinquante**
		nearly fifty

.quant à.

| *as for* | | **quant à moi** |
| | | as for me |

.sans.

without	(+ noun)	**sans espoir**
		without hope
	(+ pronoun)	**je n'irai pas sans vous**
		I won't go without you
	(+ infinitive)	**sans parler**
		without speaking
		sans s'arrêter
		without stopping

.sauf.

except for	**ils sont tous partis, sauf John** everyone left except John
barring	**sauf accidents/sauf imprévu** barring accidents/the unexpected

.selon.

according to	**selon le président** according to the President **selon moi** in my opinion

.sous.

under	(physical)	**sous la table** under the table
	(governed by)	**sous Élisabeth II** under Elizabeth II
in	(weather)	**sous la pluie** in the rain
	(idiom)	**sous peu** before long/shortly **sous la main** to hand **sous tous rapports** in all respects **sous mes yeux** before my eyes

.sur.

on/upon	(place)	**le chat est sur le toit** the cat's on the roof
off		**je l'ai pris sur l'étagère** I took it off the shelf

out of	(proportion)	**neuf sur dix** nine out of ten **une semaine sur trois** one week in three
over	(place)	**le pont sur la Loire** the bridge over the Loire
		l'emporter sur quelqu'un to prevail over someone
about	(idiom)	**une enquête sur …** an enquiry about …
at		**sur ces paroles** at these words **sur ce, il est sorti** at this he went out
by		**quatre mètres sur cinq** four metres by five
in		**sur un ton amer** in a bitter tone (of voice)

.vers.

towards	(place)	**vers le nord** towards the north
	(time)	**vers la fin du match** towards the end of the match
about	(time)	**vers 10 heures** about 10 o'clock

.voici/voilà.

here		**le voici qui vient** here he comes
there		**voilà où il demeure** that's where he lives

9. CONJUNCTIONS

Conjunctions are words or expressions which link words, phrases or clauses. They fall into two categories, coordinating conjunctions and subordinating conjunctions:

A. Coordinating Conjunctions

1. Definition

These link two similar words or groups of words, eg nouns, pronouns, adjectives, adverbs, prepositions, phrases or clauses. The principal coordinating conjunctions (or adverbs used as conjunctions) are:

et and	**mais** but	**ou** or
ou bien or (else)	**soit** either	**ni** neither
alors then	**aussi** therefore	**donc** then, therefore
puis then *(next)*	**car** for *(because)*	**or** now
cependant however	**néanmoins** nevertheless	**pourtant** yet, however
toutefois however		

il est malade mais il ne veut pas aller au lit
he's ill but he won't go to bed

il faisait beau alors il est allé se promener
it was nice weather so he went for a walk

2. Repetition

a) Some coordinating conjunctions are repeated:

soit ... soit ...	either ... or ...
ou (bien) ... ou (bien) ...	either ... or ...

prenez soit l'un soit l'autre
take one or the other

soit tu viens avec nous, soit tu restes ici mais tu te décides
either you come with us or you stay here, but you have to decide

ou tu t'habitues ou tu démissionnes
either you get used to it or you resign

ni ... ni ...   neither ... nor ...

le vieillard n'avait ni amis ni argent
the old man had neither friends nor money

b) **et** and **ou** can be repeated in texts of a literary nature:

et ... et ...   both ... and ...

ou ... ou ...   either ... or ...

elle ne cessa et de crier et de pleurer
she didn't stop shouting and crying

ou c'est lui ou c'est moi !
it's either him or me!

3. aussi

aussi means 'therefore' only when placed before the verb. The subject pronoun is placed after the verb (see p 244).

il pleuvait, aussi Pascal n'est-il pas sorti
it was raining, so Pascal didn't go out

When **aussi** follows the verb it means 'also':

j'ai aussi emporté des pulls, au cas où
I also brought some jumpers, just in case

B. Subordinating Conjunctions

These join a subordinate clause to another clause, usually a main clause.
The principal subordinating conjunctions are:

comme	as	**parce que**	because
puisque	since	**ainsi que**	(just) as
à mesure que	as	**tant que**	as long as
avant que	before	**après que**	after
jusqu'à ce que	until	**depuis que**	since
pendant que	while	**tandis que**	whereas
si	if	**à moins que**	unless
pourvu que	provided that	**quoique**	although
bien que	although	**quand**	when
lorsque	when	**dès que**	as soon as
aussitôt que	as soon as	**pour que**	in order that
afin que	so that	**de sorte que**	so that
de façon que	so that	**de peur que** (+ ne)	for fear that, lest

Note that some subordinating conjunctions require the subjunctive (see pp 137-8).

C. Que

1. Coordinating (see pp 48-9 and 59-61)

que is a coordinating conjunction when used in comparisons:

> **il est plus fort que moi**
> he is stronger than I

> **elle est plus courageuse que tu ne crois**
> she's braver than you think

2. Subordinating

a) *meaning 'that':*

> **elle dit qu'elle l'a vu**　　　**je pense que tu as raison**
> she says she has seen him　　I think you're right

> **il faut que tu viennes**　　　**il paraît qu'elle a gagné**
> you'll have to come　　　　it seems she's won

b) *replacing another conjunction:*

When a conjunction introduces more than one verb, **que** usually replaces the second subordinating conjunction and any subsequent ones to avoid repetition:

> **comme il était tard et que j'étais fatigué, je suis rentré**
> as it was late and I was tired, I went home

> **s'il fait beau et que tu es libre, nous irons à la piscine**
> if the weather's nice and you're free, we'll go to the swimming pool

> **nous sortirons lorsque nous aurons déjeuné et que tu te seras reposé**
> we'll go out when we've had lunch and you've had a rest

10. NUMBERS AND QUANTITY

A. Cardinal Numbers

0	zéro	40	quarante
1	un (une)	50	cinquante
2	deux	60	soixante
3	trois	70	soixante-dix
4	quatre	71	soixante et onze
5	cinq	72	soixante-douze
6	six	80	quatre-vingt(s)
7	sept	90	quatre-vingt-dix
8	huit	99	quatre-vingt-dix-neuf
9	neuf	100	cent
10	dix	101	cent un(e)
11	onze	102	cent deux
12	douze	121	cent vingt et un(e)
13	treize	122	cent vingt-deux
14	quatorze	200	deux cents
15	quinze	201	deux cent un(e)
16	seize	1000	mille
17	dix-sept	1988	mille neuf cent
18	dix-huit		quatre-vingt-huit
19	dix-neuf	2000	deux mille
20	vingt	10,000	dix mille
30	trente	1,000,000	un million

Note:

a) **un** is the only cardinal number which agrees with the noun in gender:

un kilo	**une pomme**
a kilo	an apple

b) hyphens are used in compound numbers between 17 and 99 except where **et** is used (this also applies to compound numbers after 100: **cent vingt-trois** 123).

c) **cent** and **mille** are not preceded by **un** as in English (one hundred).

d) **vingt** and **cent** multiplied by a number take an **s** when they are not followed by another number.

> **il a quatre-vingts ans**
> he's eighty

> **elle a remporté quatre-vingt-deux victoires**
> she has notched up eighty-two wins

> **c'est une civilisation vieille de huit cents ans**
> it's a civilization which is eight hundred years old

> **ce livre compte trois cent cinq pages**
> this book has three hundred and five pages

e) **mille** is invariable.

> **trente mille personnes ont assisté à la rencontre**
> thirty thousand people went to the match

B. Ordinal Numbers

		abbreviation
1st	premier/première	1er/1ère
2nd	deuxième/second	2^e
3rd	troisième	3^e
4th	quatrième	4^e
5th	cinquième	5^e
6th	sixième	6^e
7th	septième	7^e
8th	huitième	8^e
9th	neuvième	9^e
10th	dixième	10^e
11th	onzième	11^e
12th	douzième	12^e
13th	treizième	13^e
14th	quatorzième	14^e
15th	quinzième	15^e
16th	seizième	16^e
17th	dix-septième	17^e
18th	dix-huitième	18^e
19th	dix-neuvième	19^e
20th	vingtième	20^e
21st	vingt et unième	21^e
22nd	vingt-deuxième	22^e
30th	trentième	30^e
100th	centième	100^e
101st	cent unième	101^e
200th	deux centième	200^e
1000th	millième	1000^e
10,000th	dix millième	$10\ 000^e$

Note:

a) ordinal numbers are formed by adding **-ième** to cardinal numbers, except for **premier** and **second**; **cinq**, **neuf** and numbers ending in **e** undergo slight changes: **cinquième, neuvième, onzième, douzième** etc.

b) ordinal numbers agree with the noun in gender and number:

le Premier ministre
the Prime Minister

la première fleur
du printemps
the first flower of spring

c) there is no elision with **huitième** and **onzième**:

le huitième jour
the eighth day

du onzième candidat
of the eleventh candidate

d) cardinal numbers are used for monarchs, except for 'first':

Charles deux
Charles II

Charles premier
Charles I

C. Fractions And Proportions

1. Fractions

Fractions are expressed as in English: cardinal followed by ordinal:

deux cinquièmes
two fifths

But: $\frac{1}{4}$ **un quart** $\frac{1}{2}$ **un demi, une demie**

    $\frac{1}{3}$ **un tiers** $\frac{3}{4}$ **trois quarts**

2. Decimals

The English decimal point is conveyed by a comma in French:

un virgule huit (1,8)
one point eight (1.8)

3. Approximate numbers

une huitaine   **une dizaine**
about eight   about ten

une trentaine   **une centaine**
some thirty   about a hundred

But: **un millier**
about a thousand

Note that **de** is used when the approximate number is followed by a noun:

une vingtaine d'enfants
about twenty children

4. Arithmetic

Addition:	**deux plus quatre**	2+4
Subtraction:	**cinq moins deux**	5−2
Multiplication:	**trois fois cinq**	3×5
Division:	**six divisé par deux**	6÷2
Square:	**deux au carré**	2^2
Power:	**deux puissance six**	2^6

D. Measurements And Prices

1. Measurements

a) *Dimensions*

long(ue)/de longueur/de long	long
profond(e)/de profondeur/de profond	deep
épais(se)/d'épaisseur	thick
haut(e)/de hauteur/de haut	high

la salle de classe est longue de 12 mètres
la salle de classe a/fait 12 mètres de longueur/de long
the classroom is 12 metres long

ma chambre fait quatre mètres sur trois
my bedroom is about four metres by three

b) *Distance*

à quelle distance sommes-nous de la gare?
how far are we from the station?

nous sommes à deux kilomètres de la gare
we are two kilometres from the station

combien y a-t-il d'ici à Blois?
how far is it to Blois?

2. Price

ce pull m'a coûté 20 euros
this sweater cost me 20 euros

j'ai payé ce pull 20 euros
I paid 20 euros for this sweater

des pommes à 2 euros le kilo
apples at 2 euros a kilo

du vin blanc à 3 euros la bouteille
white wine at 3 euros a bottle

cela fait/revient à 6 euros
that comes to 6 euros

ils coûtent 4 euros pièce
they cost 4 euros each

E. Expressions Of Quantity

Quantity may be expressed by an adverb of quantity, eg 'a lot', 'too much' or by a noun which names the actual quantity involved, eg 'a bottle', 'a dozen'.

1. Expression of quantity + 'de' + noun

Before a noun, adverbs and other expressions of quantity are followed by **de** (**d'** before a vowel or a silent **h**) and never by **du, de la** or **des**, except for **bien des** and **la plupart du/des**:

assez de enough	**autant de** as much/many
beaucoup de a lot of/much/many	**combien de** how much/many
moins de less/fewer	**plus de** more
peu de little/few	**un peu de** a little
tant de so much/many	**tellement de** so much/many
bien du/de la/des many/a lot of	**la plupart du/de la/des** most
trop de too much/many	
il y a assez de fromage? is there enough cheese?	**autant de gens** as many people
je n'ai pas beaucoup de temps I haven't got much time	**il y a combien de pièces?** how many rooms are there?
j'ai mis moins de temps que lui I took less time than him	**mange plus de légumes!** eat more vegetables!
peu de gens le savent not many people know that	**tu veux un peu de pain?** would you like a little bread?
il y a tant d'années so many years ago	**j'ai tellement de travail** I've got so much work

bien des gens
a good many people

la plupart des Français
most French people

tu as bien de la patience
you have a lot of patience

il y a trop de voitures
there are too many cars

2. Noun expressing quantity + 'de' + noun

une boîte de
a box/tin/can/jar of

une bouteille de
a bottle of

une bouchée de
a mouthful of *(food)*

une cuillerée de
a spoonful of

une douzaine de
a dozen

une gorgée de
a mouthful of *(drink)*

un kilo de
a kilo of

un litre de
a litre of

une livre de
a pound of

un morceau de
a piece of

un paquet de
a packet of

une paire de
a pair of

une part de
a share/helping of

une tasse de
a cup of

une tranche de
a slice of

un verre de
a glass of

je voudrais une boîte de thon et un litre de lait
I'd like a tin of tuna and a litre of milk

il y a une boîte de limonade dans le frigo
there's a can of lemonade in the fridge

j'ai pris deux parts de choucroute
I took two helpings of sauerkraut

il a mangé une douzaine d'œufs et six morceaux de poulet
he ate a dozen eggs and six pieces of chicken

3. Expressions of quantity used without a noun

When an expression of quantity is not followed by a noun, **de** is replaced by the pronoun **en** (see pp 82-4):

> **il y avait beaucoup de neige; il y en avait beaucoup**
> there was a lot of snow; there was a lot (of it)

> **elle a mangé trop de chocolats; elle en a trop mangé**
> she's eaten too many chocolates; she's eaten too many (of them)

11. EXPRESSIONS OF TIME

A. The Time

quelle heure est-il?   what time is it?

a) *full hours*

il est midi/minuit   **il est une heure**
it is 12 noon *or* midday/midnight   it is 1 o'clock

b) *half-hours*

il est minuit et demi(e)   **il est midi et demi(e)**
it is 12.30 a.m.   it is 12.30 p.m.

il est une heure et demie
it is 1.30

c) *quarter-hours*

il est deux heures un/et quart   **il est deux heures moins**
it is a quarter past two   **le/un quart**
                                     it is a quarter to two

d) *minutes*

il est quatre heures vingt-trois **il est cinq heures moins**
it is 23 minutes past 4   **vingt**
                                      it is 20 to 5

Note that **minutes** is usually omitted; **heures** is never omitted.

e) *a.m. and p.m.*

du matin   **de l'après-midi/du soir**
a.m., in the morning   p.m., in the evening

il est sept heures moins dix   **il est sept heures dix du soir**
   du matin   it is 7.10 p.m *or* in the evening
it is 6.50 a.m. *or* in the morning

235

The 24-hour clock is commonly used:

dix heures trente
10.30 a.m.

quatorze heures trente-cinq
2.35 p.m.

dix-neuf heures dix
7.10 p.m.

Note that times are often abbreviated as follows:

dix-neuf heures dix   19h10

B. The Date

1. Names of months, days and seasons

a) *Months (les mois)*

janvier	January
février	February
mars	March
avril	April
mai	May
juin	June
juillet	July
août	August
septembre	September
octobre	October
novembre	November
décembre	December

b) *Days of the week (les jours de la semaine)*

lundi	Monday
mardi	Tuesday
mercredi	Wednesday
jeudi	Thursday
vendredi	Friday
samedi	Saturday
dimanche	Sunday

c) *Seasons (les saisons)*

le printemps	spring
l'été	summer
l'automne	autumn
l'hiver	winter

For prepositions used with the seasons see p 18.

Note that in French, months and days are masculine and do not have a capital letter unless they begin a sentence.

2. Dates

a) Cardinals (eg **deux, trois**) are used for the dates of the month except the first:

le quatorze juillet	**le deux novembre**
the fourteenth of July	the second of November

But: **le premier février**
the first of February

The definite article is used as in English; French does not use prepositions ('on' and 'of' in English):

je vous ai écrit le trois mars
I wrote to you on the third of March

b) **mil** (a thousand) is used instead of **mille** in dates from 1001 onwards:

mil neuf cent quatre-vingt sept
nineteen hundred and eighty-seven

l'an deux mil deux
the year two thousand and two

3. Année, journée, matinée, soirée

Année, journée, matinée, soirée (the feminine forms of **an, jour, matin** and **soir**) are usually found in the following cases:

a) *when duration is implied:*

pendant une année	for a (whole) year
toute la journée	all day long, the whole day
dans la matinée	in the (course of the) morning
passer une soirée	to spend an evening
l'année scolaire/universitaire	the school/academic year

b) *with an ordinal number or an indefinite expression:*

la deuxième année	the second year
dans sa vingtième année	in his twentieth year
plusieurs/quelques années	several/a few years
bien des/de nombreuses années	many years
environ une année	about a year

c) *with an adjective:*

de bonnes/mauvaises années   good/bad years

C. Idiomatic Expressions

à cinq heures	at five o'clock
à onze heures environ	(at) about eleven o'clock
vers minuit	(at) about midnight
vers (les) dix heures	(at) about ten o'clock
il est six heures passées	it's past six o'clock
à quatre heures précises/pile	at exactly four o'clock
sur le coup de trois heures	on the stroke of three
à partir de neuf heures	from nine o'clock onwards
peu avant sept heures	shortly before seven
peu après sept heures	shortly after seven
tôt ou tard	sooner or later
au plus tôt	at the earliest
au plus tard	at the latest
il est tard	it is late
il est en retard	he is late
il se lève tard	he gets up late
il est arrivé en retard	he arrived late
le train a vingt minutes de retard	the train is twenty minutes late
ma montre retarde de six minutes	my watch is six minutes slow
ma montre avance de six minutes	my watch is six minutes fast
ce soir	this evening, tonight
demain soir	tomorrow evening, tomorrow night
hier soir	yesterday evening, last night
samedi soir	Saturday evening
je sors samedi soir	I'm going out on Saturday night or evening
dans la soirée de samedi	on Saturday evening
dans la nuit de samedi (à dimanche)	during Saturday night
demain matin	tomorrow morning
hier matin	yesterday morning
lundi matin	Monday morning

j'y vais lundi matin	I'm going there on Monday morning
demain en huit	tomorrow week
le lendemain	the next day
le lendemain matin	the next morning
hier matin	yesterday morning
la semaine dernière	last week
la semaine prochaine	next week
la semaine qui vient	this coming week
je l'ai vu l'autre samedi	I saw him the other Saturday
lundi	on Monday
le lundi	on Mondays
je commence lundi	I'm starting (on) Monday
il vient le lundi	he comes on Mondays, he comes on a Monday
vient un lundi	come one Monday
un lundi sur deux	every other Monday, every second Monday
tous les lundis	every Monday
tous les lundis soirs	every Monday evening *or* night
tous mes lundis	all my Mondays
lundi en huit	a week on Monday, Monday week
lundi en quinze	a fortnight on Monday
il y a trois semaines	three weeks ago
il vient l'après-midi	he comes in the afternoon(s)
viens un après-midi	come one afternoon
une demi-heure	a half-hour, half an hour
un quart d'heure	a quarter of an hour
trois quarts d'heure	three quarters of an hour
passer son temps (à faire)	to spend one's time (doing)
perdre son temps	to waste one's time
de temps en temps	from time to time
de temps à autre	from time to time
dans les temps	on time
au début de l'après-midi/ de la soirée, en début de/ l'après-midi de soirée	in the early afternoon/ evening

je te téléphonerai au début de la matinée	I'll phone you first thing in the morning
au début du mois	at the beginning of the month
j'ai une réunion au milieu de la matinée *ou* en milieu de matinée	I have a meeting mid-morning
au milieu (du mois) de juin, (à la) mi-juin	in the middle of June, mid-June
au milieu de l'hiver	in the middle of winter, midwinter
j'ai une réunion à la fin de la matinée *ou* en fin de matinée	I have a meeting late morning
à la fin de l'hiver	at the end of the winter
on en reparlera fin janvier *ou* à la fin du mois de janvier	we'll talk about it again at the end of January
quel jour sommes-nous aujourd'hui?	what day is it today?
le combien sommes-nous aujourd'hui?	what's the date today?, what's today's date?
nous sommes/c'est le trois avril	it's the third of April
aujourd'hui nous sommes samedi	today is Saturday, it's Saturday today
vendredi 11 janvier 2002	Friday, 11 January 2002
nous nous sommes vus le vendredi 11 janvier	we saw each other on Friday, 11th January
le vendredi treize juillet	Friday the thirteenth of July
en février/au mois de février	in February/in the month of February
en février 2002	in February 2002
l'été 2002	in the summer of 2002, in summer 2002
en 2002	in 2002
dans les années soixante	in the sixties, in the 60s, in the 1960s
au début/à la fin des années soixante	in the early/late sixties
au dix-septième siècle	in the seventeenth century
au XVIIe	in the 17th century
le jour de l'An	New Year's Day

avoir treize ans	to be thirteen (years old)
être âgé de quatorze ans	to be fourteen (years old)
elle fête ses vingt ans	she's celebrating her twentieth birthday
elle a une vingtaine d'années	she's around twenty (years old)
un plan quinquennal	a five-year plan
une année bissextile	a leap year
une année civile	a calendar year
une année-lumière	a light year

12. THE SENTENCE

A. Word Order

Word order is usually the same in French as in English, except in the following cases:

1. Adjectives

Many French adjectives follow the noun (see pp 45-7):

de l'argent *italien*
(some) *Italian* money

j'ai les yeux *bleus*
I've got *blue* eyes

2. Adverbs

In simple tenses, adverbs usually follow the verb (see p 58):

j'y vais *rarement*
I *seldom* go there

il fera *bientôt* **nuit**
it will *soon* be dark

3. Object pronouns

Object pronouns usually come before the verb (see pp 79-80):

je *t'***attendrai**
I'll wait *for you*

il *la* **lui a vendue**
he sold *it* to him

4. Noun phrases

Noun phrases are formed differently in French (see pp 263-4):

une chemise en coton
a cotton shirt

le père de mon copain
my friend's father

5. Exclamations

The word order is not affected after **que** or **comme** (unlike after 'how' in English):

que tu es bête!
you *are* silly!
(how silly you are!)

qu'il fait froid!
it's so cold!

> **comme il chante mal!**
> he sings so badly!

> **comme c'est beau!**
> that's so beautiful!

6. DONT

dont must be followed by the subject of the clause it introduces; compare:

> **l'ami dont j'ai perdu l'adresse**
> the friend whose address I lost

> **l'ami dont l'adresse a changé**
> the friend whose address has changed

7. Inversion

In certain cases, the subject of a French clause is placed after the verb. Word order is effectively that of an interrogative sentence (see pp 249-50). This occurs:

a) *after the following, when they occur at the beginning of a clause:*

> **à peine**   **aussi**   **peut-être**
> hardly   therefore   maybe, perhaps

> **à peine Alain était-il sorti qu'il a commencé à pleuvoir**
> Alain had barely gone out when it started raining

> **il y avait une grève du métro, aussi a-t-il pris un taxi**
> there was an underground strike, so he took a taxi

> **peut-être vont-ils téléphoner plus tard**
> maybe they'll phone later

But: **Alain était à peine sorti qu'il a commencé à pleuvoir**

ils vont peut-être téléphoner plus tard

b) *when a verb of saying follows direct speech:*

> **'si tu veux', a répondu Marie**
> 'if you want', Marie replied

> **'attention!' a-t-elle crié**
> 'watch out!', she shouted

> **'j'espère que non', dit-il**
> 'I hope not', he said

> **'répondez!' ordonna-t-il**
> 'answer!', he ordered

B. Negative Expressions

1. Main negative words

a)

ne … pas	not
ne … point	not (*literary*)
ne … plus	no more/ longer, not … any more
ne … jamais	never
ne … rien	nothing, not … anything
ne … guère	hardly

b)

ne … personne	nobody, no one, not … anyone
ne … que	only
ne … ni (ni … ni)	neither … nor
ne … aucun(e)	no, not any, none
ne … nul(le)	no
ne … nulle part	nowhere, not … anywhere

Note:

i) **ne** becomes **n'** before a vowel or a silent **h**.

ii) **aucun** and **nul**, like other adjectives and pronouns, agree with the word they refer to; they are used only in the singular.

2. Position of negative expressions

a) *with simple tenses and with the imperative*

Negative words enclose the verb: **ne** comes before the verb, and the second part of the negative expression comes after the verb:

je ne la connais pas I don't know her	**n'insistez pas!** don't insist!
je n'ai plus d'argent I haven't any money left	**tu ne le sauras jamais** you'll never know
ne dis rien don't say anything	**il n'y a personne** no one's here
je n'avais que 3 euros I only had 3 euros	**il n'est nulle part** it isn't anywhere

THE SENTENCE

tu n'as aucun sens de l'humour you have no sense of humour	**il n'est ni bête ni crédule** he's neither stupid nor gullible

b) *with compound tenses*

With **ne ... pas** and the other expressions in list **1 a**, the word order is: **ne** + auxiliary + **pas** + past participle:

il n'est pas revenu he didn't come back	**je n'ai plus essayé** I didn't try any more
je n'avais jamais vu Paris I had never seen Paris	**on n'a rien fait** we haven't done anything

With **ne ... personne** and the other expressions in list **1 b**, the word order is: **ne** + auxiliary + past participle + **personne/que/ni** etc:

il ne l'a dit à personne he didn't tell anyone	**tu n'en as acheté qu'un?** did you only buy one?
je n'en ai aimé aucun I didn't like any of them	**il n'est allé nulle part** he hasn't gone anywhere

c) *with the infinitive*

i) **ne ... pas** and the other expressions in list **1 a** are placed together before the verb:

je préfère ne pas y aller I'd rather not go	**essaye de ne rien perdre** try not to lose anything

ii) **ne ... personne** and the other expressions in list **1 b** enclose the infinitive:

il a été surpris de ne voir personne
he was surprised not to see anybody

j'ai décidé de n'en acheter aucun
I decided not to buy any of them

d) *at the beginning of a sentence*

When **personne**, **rien**, **aucun** and **ni ... ni ...** begin a sentence, they are followed by **ne**:

personne ne le sait
nobody knows

rien n'a changé
nothing has changed

ni Paul ni Simone ne
   sont venus
neither Paul nor Simone came

aucun secours n'est arrivé
no help arrived

3. Combination of negative expressions

Negative expressions can be combined:

ne ... plus jamais
ne ... plus rien
ne ... plus personne
ne ... plus ni ... ni
ne ... plus que

ne ... jamais rien
ne ... jamais personne
ne ... jamais ni ... ni
ne ... jamais que

on ne l'a plus jamais revu
we never saw him again

il n'y a plus rien
there isn't anything left

plus personne ne viendra
no one will come any more

tu ne dis jamais rien
you never say anything

je ne bois jamais que de l'eau
I only ever drink water

je ne vois jamais personne
I never see anybody

je ne pardonnerai jamais ni n'oublierai
I will never forgive nor forget

4. Negative expressions without a verb

a) PAS

pas (not) is the most common of all negatives; it is frequently used without a verb:

tu l'aimes? – pas beaucoup
do you like it? – not much

ah non, pas lui!
oh no, not him!

non merci, pas pour moi
no thanks, not for me

un roman pas très long
not a very long novel

lui, il viendra, mais pas moi
he will come, but I won't

j'aime ça; pas toi?
I like that; don't you?

b) *NE*

ne is not used when there is no verb:

qui a crié? – personne
who shouted? – nobody

jamais de la vie!
not on your life!

rien! je ne veux rien!
nothing! I want nothing!

rien du tout
nothing at all

c) *NON*

non (no) is always used without a verb:

tu aimes la natation? – non, pas du tout
do you like swimming? – no, not at all

tu viens, oui ou non? – je crois que non
are you coming, yes or no? – I don't think so

Note that **non plus** means 'neither':

je ne le crois pas – moi non plus
I don't believe him – neither do I

je n'ai rien mangé – nous non plus
I haven't eaten anything – neither have we

C. Direct And Indirect Questions

1. Direct questions

There are three ways of forming direct questions in French:

a) *subject + verb (+ question word)*

The word order remains the same as in statements (subject + verb) but the intonation changes: the voice is raised at the end of the sentence. This is by far the most common question form in conversational French:

tu l'as acheté où?	**je peux téléphoner d'ici?**
where did you buy it?	can I phone from here?
vous prendrez quel train?	**tu me fais confiance?**
which train will you take?	do you trust me?
c'était comment?	**la gare est près d'ici?**
what was it like?	is the station near here?
le train part à quelle heure?	**cette robe me va?**
what time does the train leave?	does this dress suit me?

b) *(question word) + **est-ce que** + subject + verb*

This question form is also very common in conversation:

qu'est-ce que tu as?	**est-ce qu'il est là?**
what's the matter with you?	is he in?
est-ce que ton ami s'est amusé?	
did your friend have a good time?	
où est-ce que vous avez mal?	
where does it hurt?	

c) *inversion*

This question form is the most formal of the three, and the least commonly used in conversation:

i) If the subject is a pronoun, the word order is as follows:

    (question word) + verb + hyphen + subject

où allez-vous?	**voulez-vous commander?**
where are you going?	do you wish to order?
quand est-il arrivé?	**avez-vous bien dormi?**
when did he arrive?	did you sleep well?

ii) If the subject is a noun, a pronoun referring to the noun is inserted after the verb, and linked to it with a hyphen:

(question word) + noun subject + verb + hyphen + pronoun

où ton père travaillait-il?	**Nicole en veut-elle?**
where did your father work?	does Nicole want any?

iii) **-t-** is inserted before **il** and **elle** when the verb ends in a vowel:

comment va-t-il voyager?	**aime-t-elle le café?**
how will he travel?	does she like coffee?
pourquoi a-t-il refusé?	**Marie viendra-t-elle?**
why did he refuse?	will Marie be coming?

Note that when a question word is used, modern French will often just invert the verb and the noun subject, without adding a pronoun; no hyphen is then necessary:

où travaille ton père?
where does your father work?

2. Indirect questions

a) *Definition*

Indirect questions follow a verb and are introduced by an interrogative word, eg:

ask him when he will arrive	I don't know why he did it

b) *Word order*

i) The word order is usually the same as in statements: question word + subject + verb:

je ne sais pas s'il voudra	**dis-moi où tu l'as mis**
I don't know if he'll want to	tell me where you put it

il n'a pas dit quand il appellerait
he didn't say when he would phone

ii) If the subject is a noun, the verb and subject are sometimes inverted:

demande-leur où est le camping
ask them where the campsite is

But: **je ne comprends pas comment l'accident s'est produit**
I don't understand how the accident happened

il ne savait pas pourquoi elle avait l'air triste
he didn't know why she looked sad

3. Translation of English question tags

Examples of question tags are: isn't it? aren't you? doesn't he? won't they? haven't you? is it? did you? and so on. Question tags are not used in French as often as they are in English. Some of them can, however, be translated in the following ways:

i) **n'est-ce pas?**

n'est-ce pas? is used at the end of a sentence when confirmation of a statement is expected:

c'était très intéressant, n'est-ce pas?
it was very interesting, wasn't it?

tu voudrais partir en vacances, n'est-ce pas?
you'd like to go on holiday, wouldn't you?

vous n'arriverez pas trop tard, n'est-ce pas?
you won't be arriving too late, will you?

ii) **hein?** and **non?**

In conversation **hein?** and **non?** are often used after affirmative statements instead of **n'est-ce pas**:

il fait beau, hein?　　　　　　**il est amusant, non?**
the weather's nice, isn't it?　　　he's funny, isn't he?

D. Answers ('Yes' And 'No')

1. OUI, SI and NON

a) **oui** and **si** mean 'yes' and are equivalent to longer affirmative answers such as 'yes, it is', 'yes, I will', 'yes, he has' etc:

> **tu m'écriras? – oui, bien sûr!**
> will you write to me? – (yes) of course I will

b) **non** means 'no' and is equivalent to longer negative answers such as 'no, it isn't', 'no, I didn't' etc:

> **c'était bien? – non, on s'est ennuyé**
> was it good? – no, it wasn't, we were bored

2. OUI or SI?

oui and **si** both mean 'yes', but **oui** is used to answer an affirmative question, and **si** to contradict a negative question:

> **cette place est libre? – oui**
> is this seat free? – yes (it is)

> **tu n'aimes pas lire? – si, bien sûr!**
> don't you like reading? – yes, of course (I do)

13. TRANSLATION PROBLEMS

A. General Translation Problems

1. French words not translated in English

Some French words are not translated in English, particularly:

a) *Articles*

Definite and indefinite articles are not always translated (see pp 16-21):

> **dans** *la* **société moderne**
> in modern society

> *les* **gens en ont assez!**
> people have had enough!

> **ah non! encore** *du* **riz! je déteste** *le* **riz!**
> oh no! rice again! I hate rice!

b) *que*

que meaning 'that' as a conjunction (see p 225) or 'that'/'which'/
'whom' as a relative pronoun (see p 94) cannot be omitted in French:

> **j'espère** *que* **tu vas mieux**
> I hope you're better

> **elle pense** *que* **c'est vrai**
> she thinks it's true

> **celui** *que* **j'ai vu**
> the one I saw

> **c'est un pays** *que* **j'aime**
> it's a country I like

c) *Prepositions*

Some French verbs are followed by a preposition (+ indirect object)
when their English equivalent takes a direct object without a
preposition (see pp 204-5):

> **elle a téléphoné** *au* **médecin**
> she phoned the doctor

> **tu l'as dit** *à* **ton père?**
> did you tell your father?

d) *le*

When **le** (it) is used in an impersonal sense (see p 79), it is not translated:

oui, je *le* sais	**dis-*le*-lui**
yes, I know	tell him

2. English words not translated in French

Some English words are not translated in French, for example:

a) *Prepositions*

i) with verbs which take an indirect object in English, but a direct object in French (see pp 203-4):

tu l'as payé combien?	**écoutez cette chanson**
how much did you pay *for* it?	listen *to* this song

ii) in certain expressions (see p 238):

je viendrai te voir lundi soir
I'll come and see you *on* Monday night

b) *'can'*

'can' + verb of hearing or seeing (see p 165):

je ne vois rien!	**tu entends la musique?**
I can't see anything!	can you hear the music?

3. Other differences

a) *English phrasal verbs*

Phrasal verbs are verbs which, when followed by a preposition, take on a different meaning, eg 'to give up', 'to walk out'. They do not exist in French and are translated by simple verbs or by expressions:

to give up	to run away	to run across
abandonner	**s'enfuir**	**traverser en courant**

b) *English possessive adjectives*

English possessive adjectives (my, your etc) are translated by the

French definite article (**le/la/les**) when parts of the body are mentioned (see p 90):

brush *your* teeth	he hurt *his* foot
brosse-toi *les* **dents**	**il s'est fait mal** *au* **pied**

c) *'from'*

'from' is translated by **à** with verbs referring to taking something away (see p 206):

he hid it *from* his parents	borrow some *from* your dad
il l'a caché *à* **ses parents**	**empruntes-en** *à* **ton père**

B. Specific Translation Problems

1. Words in -ing

The English verbal form ending in **-ing** is translated in a number of ways in French:

a) *by the appropriate French tense* (see p 126):

he's speaking (present tense)	**il parle**
he was speaking (imperfect)	**il parlait**
he will be speaking (future)	**il parlera**
he has been speaking (perfect)	**il a parlé**
he had been speaking (pluperfect)	**il avait parlé**
he would be speaking (conditional)	**il parlerait**

b) *by a French present participle* (see p 156)

i) as an adjective:

un livre amusant   **c'est effrayant**
a funny book   it's frightening

ii) as a verb, with **en** (while/on/by doing something; see pp 157-8):

'ça ne fait rien', dit-il en souriant
'it doesn't matter', he said smiling

j'ai vu mes copains en sortant du lycée
I saw my friends when I was coming out of school

Note, however, that **en** + present participle cannot be used when the two verbs have different subjects, eg:

I saw my brother coming out of school
j'ai vu mon frère sortir du lycée/qui sortait du lycée

c) *by a present infinitive* (see pp 146-54):

i) after a preposition:

au lieu de rire   **avant de traverser**
instead of laughing   before crossing

ii) after verbs of perception:

je l'ai entendu appeler
I heard him calling

je l'ai vue entrer
I saw her going in

iii) after verbs of liking and disliking:

j'adore faire du camping
I love camping

tu aimes lire?
do you like reading?

iv) after verbs followed by **à** or **de**:

tu passes tout ton temps à ne rien faire
you spend all your time doing nothing

il a commencé à neiger
it started snowing

continuez à travailler
go on working

tu as envie de sortir?
do you feel like going out?

il doit finir de manger
he must finish eating

v) when an English verb in **-ing** is the subject of another verb:

attendre serait inutile
waiting would be pointless

écrire est une corvée!
writing is a real chore!

vi) when an English verb in **-ing** follows 'is' or 'was' etc:

mon passe-temps favori, c'est de lire
my favourite pastime is reading

d) *by a perfect infinitive* (see p 154-5)

i) after **après** (after):

j'ai pris une douche après avoir nettoyé ma chambre
I had a shower after cleaning my room

ii) after certain verbs:

regretter
to regret

remercier de
to thank for

se souvenir de
to remember

j'ai regretté de leur en avoir parlé
I regretted speaking to them about it

il m'a remercié d'être allé le chercher
he thanked me for going to pick him up

e) *by a noun*

particularly when referring to sports, activities, hobbies etc:

le ski	la natation	l'équitation
skiing	swimming	horse-riding

la voile	le patinage	le canoë
sailing	skating	canoeing

la lecture	la planche à voile	la cuisine
reading	windsurfing	cooking

la boxe	la lutte	la marche à pied
boxing	wrestling	walking

2. IT IS (IT'S)

'it is' (it's) can be translated in three ways in French:

a) *il or elle* (see p 78)

il or **elle** are used with the verb **être** to translate 'it is', 'it was' etc (+ adjective) when referring to a particular masculine or feminine noun (a thing, a place etc):

> **merci de ta carte; elle était très amusante**
> thanks for your card; it was very funny

> **regarde ce blouson; il n'est vraiment pas cher**
> look at this jacket; it really isn't that expensive

b) *ce* (see pp 64-5)

ce (**c'** before a vowel) is used with the verb **être** to translate 'it is', 'it was' etc in two cases:

i) If **être** is followed by a word which is not an adjective on its own, ie by a noun, a pronoun, an expression of place etc:

c'était ta voix	**c'est une grande maison**
it was your voice	it's a big house

c'est moi! c'est Claude!	**c'est le tien?**
it's me! it's Claude!	is it yours?

c'est en France que tu vas?   **c'est pour lundi**
is it France you're going to?   it's for Monday

ii) If **être** is followed by an adjective which refers to something previously mentioned, such as an idea, an event or a fact, but not to a specific noun:

l'homme n'ira jamais sur Saturne; ce n'est pas possible
Man will never go to Saturn; it's not possible

j'ai passé mes vacances en Italie; c'était formidable!
I spent my holidays in Italy; it was great!

oh, je m'excuse! – ce n'est pas grave
oh, I'm sorry! – it's all right

c) *il* (see pp 122-5)

il is used to translate 'it is', 'it was' etc in three cases:

i) With **être** followed by an adjective + **de** or **que**, ie referring to something that follows, but not to a specific noun:

il est impossible de connaître l'avenir
it's impossible to know the future

il est évident que tu ne me crois pas
it's obvious you don't believe me

ii) To describe the weather (see p 122):

il y a du vent   **il faisait très froid**
it's windy   it was very cold

iii) With **être** to tell the time and in phrases relating to the time of day, or in such expressions as **il est temps de** (it's time to):

il est deux heures du matin   **il est tard!**
it's two in the morning   it's late!

il est temps de partir
it's time to go

Note that with other expressions of time, **c'est** is used:

c'est lundi ou mardi aujourd'hui?   **c'était l'été**
is it Monday or Tuesday today?   it was summer

3. TO BE

Although 'to be' is usually translated by **être**, it can also be translated in the following ways:

a) *avoir*

i) **avoir** is used instead of **être** in many set expressions:

avoir faim/soif	to be hungry/thirsty
avoir chaud/froid	to be warm/cold
avoir peur/honte	to be afraid/ashamed
avoir tort/raison	to be wrong/right

ii) **avoir** is also used for age:

quel âge as-tu?	**j'ai vingt-cinq ans**
how old are you?	I'm twenty-five

b) *aller*

aller is used for describing health:

je vais mieux	**tout le monde va bien**
I am/feel better	everyone's fine

c) *faire*

faire is used in many expressions to describe the weather (see p 122):

il fait beau	**il fera chaud**
the weather's nice	it will be hot

Note that **il y a** can also be used to describe the weather, but only before **du/de la/des**:

il y a du vent/des nuages/de la tempête
it's windy/cloudy/stormy

d) *untranslated*

'to be' is not translated when it is the first part of an English continuous tense; instead, the appropriate tense is used in French (see p 126):

I'm having a bath	he was driving slowly
je prends un bain	**il conduisait lentement**

4. ANY

'any' can be translated in three different ways:

a) *du/de la/des* or *de* (see pp 22-3)

The partitive article is used with a noun in negative and interrogative sentences:

il ne mange jamais de viande
he never eats meat

tu veux du pain?
do you want any bread?

b) *en* (see p 83)

en is used to translate 'any' when it occurs without a noun in negative and interrogative sentences:

je n'en ai pas
I haven't got any

il en reste?
is there any left?

c) *n'importe quel(le)s/quel(le)s* or *tout(e)/tou(te)s*

these are used to translate 'any' (and 'every') when they mean 'no matter which':

il pourrait arriver à n'importe quel moment
he could arrive any time

prends n'importe quelle couleur, je les aime toutes
take any colour, I like them all

5. ANYONE, ANYTHING, ANYWHERE

Like 'any', these can be translated in different ways:

a) *in interrogative sentences:*

il y a quelqu'un?
is anyone in?

tu l'as vu quelque part?
did you see it anywhere?

il a dit quelque chose?
did he say anything?

b) *in negative sentences:*

il n'y a personne
there isn't anyone

je ne le vois nulle part
I can't see it anywhere

je n'ai rien fait
I didn't do anything

c) *in the sense of 'any' (and 'every'), 'no matter which':*

n'importe qui peut le faire
anyone can do that

il croit n'importe quoi
he believes anything

j'irai n'importe où
I'll go anywhere

n'importe quand
anytime

6. YOU, YOUR, YOURS, YOURSELF

French has two separate sets of words to translate 'you', 'your', 'yours', 'yourself':

a) **tu, te (t'), toi, ton/ta/tes, le tien** etc
b) **vous, votre/vos, le vôtre** etc

For their respective meanings and uses, see pp 77-8, 85-6, 89-90, 91-2.

a) *tu etc*

tu, te, ton etc correspond to the **tu** form of the verb (second person singular) and are used when speaking to one person you know well (a friend, a relative) or to someone younger. They represent the familiar form of address:

**si *tu* viens au concert avec *ton* copain, je *t'*achète
deux places; une pour *toi* et une pour lui**
if *you*'re coming to the concert with *your* boyfriend,
I'll get *you* two tickets; one for *you* and one for him

b) *vous etc*

vous, vos etc correspond to the **vous** form of the verb (second person plural) and are used:

i) when speaking to more than one person:

dépêchez-*vous*, les gars! *Vous* allez manquer le train
hurry up, boys! *You*'ll miss the train

ii) when speaking to one person you do not know well or to someone older. They represent the formal or polite form of address:

je regrette, Monsieur, mais *vous* ne pouvez pas garder *votre* chien avec *vous* dans ce restaurant
I'm sorry, sir, but *you* can't keep *your* dog with *you* in this restaurant

c) when speaking or writing to one person, you must not mix words from both sets, but decide whether you are being formal or familiar, and use the same form of address throughout:

**Cher Michel,
   Merci de ta lettre. Comment vas-*tu*? ...**
Dear Michel,
   Thanks for *your* letter. How are *you*? ...

**Monsieur,
   Pourriez-vous me réserver une chambre dans *votre* hôtel pour le 8 juin?**
Dear Sir,
   Could *you* book a room for me in *your* hotel for 8th June?

vous etc and **tu** etc can only be used together when **vous** is plural (ie when it refers to more than one person):

tu **sais, Jean,** *toi* **et** *ta* **sœur,** *vous vous* **ressemblez**
you know, Jean, *you* and *your* sister look like *each other*

7. Noun phrases

A noun phrase is a combination of two nouns used together to name things or people. In English, the first of these nouns is used to describe the second one, eg 'a love story'. In French, however, the position of the two nouns is reversed, so that the describing noun comes second and is linked to the first one by the preposition **de** (or **d'**):

une histoire d'amour
a love story

une feuille d'impôts
a tax form

un magasin de disques
a record shop

un acteur de cinéma
a film actor

un arrêt d'autobus
a bus stop

un film d'aventure
an adventure film

un coup de soleil	**une boule de neige**
sunstroke	a snowball
un roman de science-fiction	**un match de football**
a science-fiction novel	a football match
le château d'Édimbourg	**un conte de fées**
Edinburgh castle	a fairy tale
un joueur de rugby	**un employé de bureau**
a rugby player	an office worker

Note that when the describing noun refers to a type of material, the preposition **en** is often used instead of **de**:

un pull en laine	**un pantalon en cuir**
a woollen jumper	leather trousers
une bague en or	**un sac en plastique**
a gold ring	a plastic bag

8. Possession

In English, possession is often expressed by using a noun phrase and tagging **'s** at the end of the first word, eg:

> my friend's cat

This is translated in French by: object + **de** + possessor:

> **le chat de mon ami**

Note the use of the article **le/la/les**.

le fiancé de ma sœur	**les amis de Claire**
my sister's fiancé	Claire's friends
les événements de la semaine dernière	
last week's events	

When **'s** is used to refer to someone's house or shop etc, it is translated by the preposition **chez**:

je téléphone de chez Paul	**chez le dentiste**
I'm telephoning from Paul's (house)	at/to the dentist's

INDEX

INDEX